EXPLORING THE DEPTHS OF ASSEMBLY AND MACHINE LANGUAGE

Expert-Level Techniques for
Writing Efficient, Low-Level Code
for Modern Architectures

NATHAN WESTWOOD

TABLE OF CONTENTS

ABOUT THE AUTHOR!

Dr. Nathan Westwood

Biography:

Dr. Nathan Westwood is a pioneering technologist known for his exceptional contributions to the fields of software development, cloud computing, and artificial intelligence. With a passion for innovation and a relentless drive to solve complex problems, Nathan has become a prominent figure in the tech industry, shaping the future of digital technology.

Born and raised in Silicon Valley, Nathan's interest in technology started at a young age. His fascination with computers and coding led him to pursue a degree in Computer Science from Stanford University, where he excelled academically and honed his skills in programming and software engineering. During his time at Stanford, Nathan was involved in several cutting-edge projects that sparked his interest in AI and cloud technologies.

After graduating, Nathan joined a leading tech firm where he played a key role in developing cloud-based solutions that revolutionized data storage and analytics. His work in the early stages of cloud computing set the foundation for modern infrastructure-as-a-service (IaaS) platforms, earning him recognition as one of the industry's emerging stars. As a lead engineer, Nathan was instrumental in launching products that have since become industry standards.

Nathan's entrepreneurial spirit led him to co-found his own tech startup focused on AI-driven automation tools for businesses. Under his leadership, the company rapidly gained traction, attracting both investors and clients who were eager to leverage his innovative AI solutions to streamline operations and improve efficiency. Nathan's commitment to pushing the boundaries of what's possible in tech quickly earned him a reputation as a visionary leader.

Known for his expertise in machine learning, Nathan has also worked with several large tech companies, advising on the integration of AI and data science into their operations. His work has spanned various sectors, including healthcare, finance, and manufacturing, where he has helped organizations harness the power of data and automation to achieve exponential growth.

Beyond his technical achievements, Nathan is a sought-after speaker at global tech conferences, where he shares his insights on the future of cloud computing, artificial intelligence, and the ethical challenges posed by emerging technologies. His thought leadership and commitment to ethical innovation have made him a respected voice in the tech community.

In addition to his professional accomplishments, Nathan is deeply passionate about mentoring the next generation of tech leaders. He regularly contributes to educational programs and initiatives designed to inspire young minds and equip them with the skills necessary to thrive in the ever-evolving tech landscape.

Nathan Westwood continues to be a trailblazer in the tech industry, shaping the future of technology with his innovative ideas, entrepreneurial spirit, and commitment to making a positive impact on the world.

CHAPTER 1: INTRODUCTION TO LOW-LEVEL PROGRAMMING

Overview: The Role of Low-Level Programming in Modern Computing

Low-level programming refers to writing software that communicates directly with the hardware of a computer. Unlike high-level languages, such as Python or Java, which abstract away the underlying hardware complexity, low-level languages like Assembly and Machine Language operate close to the hardware layer. This proximity gives developers fine-grained control over system resources, enabling them to optimize performance, manage memory efficiently, and even interact directly with hardware components like processors and memory devices.

In modern computing, low-level programming plays an essential role despite the prevalence of high-level languages that offer ease of use and rapid application development. Low-level programming is the backbone of systems programming, where efficiency and direct hardware manipulation are paramount. Operating systems, device drivers, embedded systems, and other critical software components often rely on low-level code to ensure fast, reliable, and resource-efficient operations.

At the core of low-level programming are two main languages: **Assembly Language** and **Machine Language**. Both are often used interchangeably when discussing low-level programming but serve different purposes within the ecosystem. Understanding their role in modern computing, especially as hardware continues to evolve, is vital for developers who aim to master the art of performance tuning, system optimization, and hardware-specific programming.

In this chapter, we will explore what low-level programming entails, its significance in computing, and the practical applications where it thrives. We'll set the stage for the subsequent chapters that delve into Assembly and Machine Language, providing you with the foundational knowledge needed to excel in this space.

The Assembly and Machine Language Connection

Low-level programming revolves around the interaction between software and hardware. The two primary languages used in this domain—**Assembly Language** and **Machine Language**—are the closest forms of code that speak directly to a computer's hardware. To truly understand the role of low-level programming, it's essential to comprehend how these languages communicate with the machine at its core.

1. Machine Language: The Foundation of All Computing

Machine language is the most fundamental level of programming, consisting of binary code—1s and 0s—that the computer's processor can directly execute. Every operation performed by the CPU, whether it's an arithmetic calculation or memory retrieval, boils down to a binary instruction. These binary instructions are the machine's native language, often referred to as **opcode** (operation code). Each processor architecture—x86, ARM, RISC-V, etc.—has its own unique set of machine instructions, tailored to its design and capabilities.

Machine code is tightly bound to the specific architecture of the hardware. For example, a machine instruction for an Intel processor will differ from that of an ARM processor. While high-level languages are abstracted from hardware and are portable across different machines, machine language is strictly tied to a particular type of processor.

Writing in machine language directly is exceedingly difficult for humans because it involves manipulating raw binary code. However, **Assembly Language** serves as a bridge between the human-readable format and machine code, providing mnemonics and shorthand notations to represent machine instructions.

2. **Assembly Language: Human-Readable, Machine-Executable**

Assembly Language is a symbolic representation of machine language. It replaces binary opcodes with easily recognizable mnemonics like MOV (move), ADD (add), and JMP (jump). These mnemonics are designed to be more understandable than raw binary, yet they still translate directly into machine code. While high-level programming languages provide significant abstraction, Assembly allows programmers to write code that is almost as close to the hardware as machine language itself.

For example, a simple Assembly command might look like this:

```
nginx

MOV AX, 1    ; Load the value 1 into register AX
```

This line tells the processor to load the value 1 into a specific register, **AX**. In contrast, the machine code that corresponds to this operation is a binary representation that the CPU can understand directly.

While Assembly provides a more human-friendly approach, it's still highly dependent on the underlying hardware. For example, the syntax and available instructions in Assembly will vary between different CPU architectures, which means that Assembly code written for an Intel x86 processor won't run on an ARM-based system without modifications.

By understanding Assembly, a developer gains insight into the inner workings of the CPU and memory, enabling them to write highly efficient, optimized code.

Real-World Applications: Industries That Rely on Assembly and Machine Languages

Despite the rise of high-level programming languages, low-level programming remains indispensable in several industries that demand maximum performance, reliability, and efficiency. Let's explore some of the key sectors that rely heavily on low-level languages like Assembly and Machine Language.

1. Embedded Systems and IoT

Embedded systems are specialized computing systems that do not look like typical general-purpose computers. They are typically designed to perform specific tasks and are often constrained by resource limitations like memory, processing power, and energy consumption. Embedded systems power a vast array of devices, from household appliances to industrial machinery, and even smart devices in the Internet of Things (IoT).

For example, a microcontroller used in a washing machine must interact with sensors, motors, and other hardware components to ensure the correct operation of the appliance. To achieve this, engineers write low-level code in Assembly to control the hardware precisely and ensure the system runs efficiently.

In many embedded systems, high-level languages like Python or JavaScript are not feasible due to their overhead, making Assembly or Machine Language the preferred choice for developers who need complete control over system resources.

2. **Operating Systems**

An operating system (OS) is the backbone of any computer system. It controls hardware, manages resources, and provides services for application software. The OS needs to be fast, reliable, and capable of handling complex tasks like memory management, process scheduling, and device control.

Although much of modern operating system development is done in higher-level languages like C, key parts of the OS, such as device drivers and bootloaders, still rely on low-level programming. These components must interact directly with the hardware and execute efficiently with minimal overhead, which is why Assembly remains relevant in the development of operating systems.

3. **Gaming and Graphics Programming**

Video games are another domain where low-level programming shines. High-performance games require fast and responsive interactions with hardware, including graphics rendering, physics calculations, and input/output handling. Developers who create game engines or work on graphics-heavy games must have an in-depth understanding of how hardware works at the Assembly level.

In graphics programming, for instance, Assembly code can be used to fine-tune how a game interacts with the graphics processing unit (GPU), improving rendering speeds and optimizing memory usage. This is especially crucial for real-time rendering in 3D games, where every frame must be generated efficiently to maintain smooth gameplay.

4. **Cybersecurity**

Low-level programming is also indispensable in the field of cybersecurity. Security experts often need to analyze and understand the underlying code of programs to identify vulnerabilities or exploits. Malware analysis, for instance, involves reverse engineering malicious software, often requiring knowledge of Assembly and Machine Language.

Exploit development also relies on low-level skills. Many vulnerabilities in software, such as buffer overflows or privilege escalation attacks, are rooted in low-level code. Hackers exploit these vulnerabilities by writing precise Assembly code to manipulate memory and system processes.

5. **Performance-Critical Applications**

Some applications require the utmost performance and cannot afford the overhead of high-level languages. These include scientific computing, financial algorithms, and other data-intensive tasks where milliseconds matter.

For example, scientific simulations used in climate modeling or fluid dynamics often need to run on supercomputers and require highly optimized code that directly interacts with hardware. In such cases, developers write performance-critical routines in Assembly to maximize speed and reduce resource consumption.

Setting Expectations: What to Expect Throughout the Book

This book aims to guide you through the exciting world of low-level programming, equipping you with the knowledge and tools to write efficient, optimized code that interacts directly with hardware. By the end of this journey, you will have a solid understanding of both **Assembly Language** and **Machine Language**, and how they are used to build high-performance systems.

Here's what you can expect as you progress through the book:

1. **Foundational Knowledge**: We'll start with the basics, ensuring you have a solid grasp of low-level programming fundamentals before diving deeper into more complex topics.
2. **Hands-on Examples**: Throughout the book, we will walk through real-world examples and hands-on projects that showcase how low-level programming is applied in different industries.
3. **Step-by-Step Guidance**: Each chapter will guide you through practical coding exercises, breaking down complex concepts into digestible steps. Whether you're writing your first line of Assembly or optimizing a piece of code for performance, you will always know exactly what to do next.
4. **Expert Techniques**: As you progress, you will learn expert-level techniques for debugging, optimizing, and writing code

that interacts directly with hardware. You'll gain the skills needed to troubleshoot issues that arise in low-level programming, making you an indispensable resource for any team working with hardware-intensive systems.

5. **Real-World Relevance**: We'll keep everything grounded in real-world applications, showing how low-level programming underpins the software and systems that power everything from smartphones to embedded devices to supercomputers.

By the end of the book, you'll be well-equipped to tackle any low-level programming challenge, confident in your ability to write code that interacts efficiently with modern architectures. You will understand how Assembly and Machine Language have shaped the world of computing and continue to play a pivotal role in areas where speed, efficiency, and direct hardware control are paramount.

CHAPTER 2: A DEEP DIVE INTO MACHINE LANGUAGE

What is Machine Language? The Binary Code That Directly Interacts with Hardware

Machine language is the lowest-level programming language, one that directly communicates with the hardware of a computer. At its core, machine language consists entirely of binary code—ones and zeros—that tell the computer's processor exactly what to do. This binary code is executed by the Central Processing Unit (CPU), the brain of the computer, and can control everything from data movement to mathematical calculations.

To understand machine language, let's first explore what "binary" means. The binary number system uses only two symbols: **0** and **1**. These two symbols, or bits, are the fundamental building blocks of all information in computing. In machine language, each command the computer follows is represented as a sequence of bits. The CPU reads this sequence, decodes it, and then takes action based on the instructions embedded in the binary code.

Machine language instructions are tightly linked to the hardware architecture of the computer. This means that a machine language instruction written for one processor type—say, an Intel processor—won't necessarily work for a different type, like an ARM processor. Each processor type has its own set of binary instructions known as its **instruction set architecture (ISA)**. The ISA defines the binary codes the processor understands and how the CPU performs operations such as arithmetic, logic, memory access, and branching.

At the most fundamental level, machine language can perform tasks such as:

- **Loading data**: Moving information from memory into registers, where the processor can access it quickly.
- **Performing arithmetic operations**: Executing addition, subtraction, multiplication, and division directly on numbers stored in memory or registers.
- **Control flow**: Managing the flow of execution, for example, deciding whether to jump to another part of the program or continue executing the next instruction.
- **Interacting with input/output devices**: Managing communication between the CPU and peripherals like keyboards, monitors, and disk drives.

The binary code, while fundamental, is extremely difficult for humans to read or write directly. This is why **Assembly language** was developed—Assembly provides a more readable way to represent the instructions that the processor can execute, but it is still very closely tied to machine language.

How the CPU Executes Machine Code

The CPU is the heart of the machine, responsible for executing all machine code instructions. When you write software, whether in a high-level language or low-level language, your program eventually needs to be translated into machine code that the CPU can execute. To understand how this happens, it's important to take a step back and examine the CPU's core components and how it processes instructions.

1. **Fetch**: The CPU retrieves instructions from memory. In modern computers, the CPU has a special register called the **Program Counter (PC)**, which keeps track of where the next instruction is located in memory. The CPU fetches the instruction pointed to by the PC.
2. **Decode**: Once the instruction is fetched, the CPU decodes it to understand what operation it needs to perform. The decoding process breaks the instruction down into parts, such as the opcode (the operation to perform) and the operands (the data or memory locations the operation will use).
3. **Execute**: The CPU performs the operation specified by the instruction. For example, if the instruction is an addition operation, the CPU will retrieve the operands (numbers), perform the addition, and store the result in a register or memory location.
4. **Store**: After the CPU executes the instruction, the result may be stored back in memory or in one of the CPU's registers for further processing.

This basic cycle is often referred to as the **Fetch-Decode-Execute (FDE)** cycle. It repeats continuously, with the CPU fetching, decoding, and executing instructions in a never-ending loop as long as the program is running.

Key Components of the CPU Involved in Execution:

- **Registers**: These are small, fast storage locations within the CPU. Registers temporarily hold data, addresses, or instruction components during execution. For example, the **Accumulator (AC)** register may hold the result of a calculation, while the **Instruction Register (IR)** holds the current instruction being executed.

- **ALU (Arithmetic Logic Unit)**: The ALU performs mathematical calculations (addition, subtraction) and logical operations (AND, OR, NOT). It is a core part of the CPU and performs the actual computations based on the instructions fetched from memory.
- **Control Unit**: The control unit directs the operation of the processor. It interprets the instructions from memory and sends the appropriate signals to the ALU, registers, and other components to carry out the operation. The Control Unit is responsible for coordinating the entire fetch-decode-execute cycle.
- **Clock**: The clock controls the timing of the CPU, sending out regular pulses that synchronize the fetching and execution of instructions. The speed of the clock (measured in Hertz) plays a significant role in the overall performance of the CPU.

Machine Code vs High-Level Languages: Key Differences and When to Use Each

Machine code and high-level programming languages serve different purposes, and each has its place in the world of computing. Let's break down the key differences between them and explore when one is more appropriate than the other.

1. **Human Readability**:
   - **Machine Code**: Machine code is purely binary, consisting of ones and zeros. This makes it incredibly difficult for humans to write or debug directly.
   - **High-Level Languages**: High-level languages, like Python, Java, and C++, are designed to be human-readable. They use English-like syntax and abstract

away the complexities of interacting directly with hardware.

2. **Level of Abstraction**:
   - o **Machine Code**: Machine code operates at the lowest level of abstraction, directly controlling hardware. It is often tailored to a specific processor architecture, meaning machine code for one CPU might not work on another.
   - o **High-Level Languages**: High-level languages offer greater abstraction, making them easier to use. They manage memory, data types, and hardware interaction behind the scenes, so the programmer doesn't need to worry about the specific details of hardware.

3. **Portability**:
   - o **Machine Code**: Machine code is not portable. Each processor type has its own machine language, which means that a program written for one type of CPU will not run on a different type without modification.
   - o **High-Level Languages**: High-level languages are designed to be portable across different platforms. With the right compiler or interpreter, code written in a high-level language can run on many different systems without modification.

4. **Performance**:
   - o **Machine Code**: Since machine code is executed directly by the CPU, it generally offers superior performance. There is no need for translation or interpretation, which means faster execution times.
   - o **High-Level Languages**: While high-level languages are more flexible and easier to write, they introduce additional layers of abstraction, which can slow down performance. Modern compilers and interpreters optimize high-level code to improve execution speed, but it still tends to be slower than machine code in performance-critical applications.

5. **Ease of Use**:

- Machine Code: Writing machine code requires deep knowledge of the CPU's architecture and the binary instruction set it uses. It is time-consuming and error-prone to write directly in machine code.
- High-Level Languages: High-level languages are much easier to learn and use, thanks to their readability and abstraction. They are designed for productivity and making complex systems manageable.

When to Use Machine Code:

Machine code is used when maximum performance is required, especially in systems where resources like memory and processing power are limited. This is common in **embedded systems**, **real-time applications**, and **device drivers**, where low-level programming is needed to ensure fast, efficient operation. If you're writing software that must interact directly with hardware or if you are designing systems where every bit of performance matters, machine code is your tool.

When to Use High-Level Languages:

For most applications, high-level languages are the go-to choice. High-level languages are ideal for creating desktop applications, web applications, and even most system software, thanks to their productivity and ease of use. When performance is less critical, high-level languages offer rapid development cycles and easier maintenance.

Hands On Example: Translating a Simple High-Level Program into Machine Code

Now that we understand the key differences between machine code and high-level languages, let's take a look at how you can translate a simple high-level program into machine code. We will go through this process step by step, using an example.

Example: Adding Two Numbers

We'll start with a simple high-level program written in C to add two numbers:

c

```
#include <stdio.h>

int main() {
    int a = 5;
    int b = 10;
    int result = a + b;
    printf("Result: %d\n", result);
    return 0;
}
```

This C program is easy to read and understand. It declares two integers, adds them together, and prints the result. However, this code needs to be translated into machine code before it can be executed by the CPU.

Step 1: Compilation

The first step is to compile the C program into machine code. The C compiler takes the high-level code and translates it into an intermediate representation, which is often in assembly language or an intermediate bytecode format. The compiler then assembles it into machine code for the specific architecture.

For example, a C compiler (such as GCC) will take the code and generate assembly code like this:

```
assembly

mov eax, 5   ; Load 5 into the EAX register
mov ebx, 10  ; Load 10 into the EBX register
add eax, ebx ; Add the values in EAX and EBX and
store the result in EAX
mov ecx, eax ; Move the result from EAX into ECX
; Now, ECX contains the result
```

Step 2: Assembly to Machine Code

The assembly code then gets translated into machine code by an assembler. Each assembly instruction is converted into binary opcodes. For example, the `mov eax, 5` instruction might be represented as:

```
10111000 00000101
```

This binary sequence is the machine code that the CPU can execute directly.

Step 3: Execution

Once the program is compiled into machine code, it can be executed by the CPU. During execution, the CPU will fetch the machine code instructions, decode them, and perform the operations specified—adding the two numbers in our example and printing the result.

In this example, the high-level C code gets translated into assembly and then into machine code, which is executed by the CPU to perform the desired operation.

Conclusion

Machine language, while difficult for humans to work with directly, is the foundation of all computing. It provides the means for the CPU to interact directly with hardware, executing tasks that are crucial to the operation of a computer. Understanding machine code, how the CPU executes it, and the key differences between high-level languages and machine language gives you a strong foundation in low-level programming. As you progress through the book, you'll learn how to take advantage of machine language's performance benefits and gain insight into the intricate workings of your computer's hardware.

CHAPTER 3:
UNDERSTANDING
ASSEMBLY LANGUAGE

What is Assembly Language? The Human-Readable Counterpart of Machine Language

Assembly language is the bridge between machine language and human-readable code. While machine language consists of binary instructions that are executed by a CPU, assembly language is a human-readable version of those instructions. It's the closest you can get to programming the computer at a very low level without dealing with binary code directly.

In machine language, each instruction is written in binary (combinations of 0s and 1s), and while this is efficient for the computer, it is not practical for humans to write or debug directly. Assembly language solves this problem by replacing binary opcodes with symbolic names called **mnemonics**. These mnemonics are short, easily understood codes that represent machine language instructions, such as `MOV`, `ADD`, and `JMP`.

An assembly language program is specific to a computer's architecture. Every CPU family, whether Intel, ARM, or MIPS, has its own assembly language syntax and set of instructions, so assembly code written for one processor won't work on another without modifications. However, assembly is still significantly more human-friendly than writing directly in machine language.

Assembly language serves as the lowest level of abstraction for programming. While high-level programming languages like Python or Java shield the programmer from understanding how the processor works, assembly language exposes the underlying hardware. By using assembly, a developer can precisely control how data is processed, how memory is used, and how hardware devices are accessed.

Common Assembly Instructions: A Breakdown of Essential Instructions Like MOV, ADD, JMP

Assembly language consists of a set of instructions that correspond directly to machine code operations. These instructions can control the flow of a program, perform calculations, move data, and handle input/output operations. Let's break down some of the most common assembly instructions that are essential for writing effective low-level code.

1. **MOV (Move)**
    The MOV instruction is one of the most fundamental instructions in assembly. It's used to data from one location to another, whether from one register to another or from memory to a register. For example:

    ```assembly
    assembly

    MOV AX, 5    ; Move the value 5 into the AX
    register
    MOV BX, AX   ;  the value from AX into BX
    ```

The `MOV` instruction does not perform any arithmetic or logical operations; it simply moves or copies data between registers, memory locations, or between the two.

2. **ADD (Addition)**

   The `ADD` instruction is used to add two values together. The result is stored in one of the operands. In most cases, one of the operands is a register, and the other can be a value or another register. Here's an example:

   ```assembly
   ADD AX, 10    ; Add the value 10 to the contents of register AX
   ADD AX, BX    ; Add the value in register BX to the value in AX
   ```

   The `ADD` instruction updates the destination operand with the sum of the operands.

3. **SUB (Subtraction)**

   Like `ADD`, the `SUB` instruction performs arithmetic, but instead of adding two values together, it subtracts the second operand from the first one. Example:

   ```assembly
   SUB AX, 5    ; Subtract 5 from the contents of AX and store the result in AX
   ```

4. **JMP (Jump)**

   The `JMP` instruction is used for controlling the flow of a program. It directs the program to jump to another part of the code, which can either be unconditional or conditional (depending on other instructions like `JE` or `JNE`). For example:

```assembly
JMP 100          ; Jump to instruction at memory
location 100
```

A `JMP` instruction is essential for creating loops, conditional branches, and function calls.

5. **CMP (Compare)**

    The `CMP` instruction is used to compare two values. It subtracts one value from another but doesn't store the result. Instead, it sets the **flags** (special registers) based on the result. These flags can then be tested using conditional jump instructions like `JE` (Jump if Equal) or `JNE` (Jump if Not Equal).

```assembly
CMP AX, BX       ; Compare the contents of AX and
BX
JE 50            ; Jump to memory address 50 if AX
== BX
```

6. **PUSH and POP**

    The `PUSH` and `POP` instructions are used for stack operations. The stack is a region of memory used to store temporary data such as function arguments, local variables, and return addresses. `PUSH` places data onto the stack, and `POP` removes data from the stack.

```assembly
PUSH AX          ; Push the contents of AX onto the
stack
POP BX           ; Pop the top value from the stack
into BX
```

7. **NOP (No Operation)**

    The `NOP` instruction does nothing—it's simply a placeholder.

While it doesn't change the state of the CPU, it's useful in debugging, padding code, and providing space for future instructions. For example:

```assembly
NOP           ; No operation (do nothing)
```

Registers and Memory: How Assembly Manipulates the CPU's Registers and Memory

Registers and memory are key components of how assembly language interacts with a computer's hardware. Registers are small, high-speed storage locations located directly within the CPU, whereas memory refers to the larger, slower storage space used by the system.

1. **Registers**
   Registers are extremely fast, hardware-level storage locations within the CPU used to temporarily hold data that is being processed. There are different types of registers, each with a specific role. Here are a few examples of general-purpose registers in the x86 architecture:
   - **AX (Accumulator)**: Often used for arithmetic operations.
   - **BX (Base)**: Used for addressing data in memory.
   - **CX (Count)**: Typically used as a loop counter.
   - **DX (Data)**: Used for input/output operations and arithmetic.

   Registers can hold immediate data values (such as constants) or memory addresses. For instance:

```assembly
MOV AX, 10     ; Move the constant 10 into
register AX
MOV BX, AX     ;  the value in AX into BX
```

2. **Memory**

   Memory is where data is stored when it is not being actively processed by the CPU. Assembly language allows direct manipulation of memory addresses using pointers. For example, loading a value from memory into a register or storing a register value into memory.

   o **Direct Memory Access**: Assembly allows you to directly access specific memory locations using **memory addressing modes**. You can load data from a given address or store data at that address.

```assembly
MOV AX, [1000h]    ; Move the value at memory
address 1000h into AX
MOV [2000h], AX    ; Store the value in AX into
memory address 2000h
```

   o **Memory Segmentation**: In some architectures (such as x86), memory is divided into segments like **code**, **data**, **stack**, and **heap**. Assembly instructions can target specific segments using special segment registers like **CS** (code segment), **DS** (data segment), and **SS** (stack segment).

```assembly
MOV DS, 0x2000    ; Set the data segment
register to 0x2000
```

3. **Working with Pointers and Addresses**

   Assembly allows you to manipulate pointers directly, which are variables that store memory addresses. For instance, you can use registers to hold the address of a memory location and then access the contents at that address.

assembly

```
LEA AX, [1000h]    ; Load the address 1000h
into AX (not the data, just the address)
MOV BX, [AX]       ; Move the value at the
address stored in AX into BX
```

Hands-on Example: Writing a Simple Assembly Program to Add Two Numbers

Now that we have explored some of the basic instructions and concepts in assembly language, let's write a simple program to add two numbers together using assembly language. This example will provide a deeper understanding of how these instructions work together in a practical scenario.

The goal of this program is to add two numbers and store the result in a register. Here's the program written in x86 assembly language:

assembly

```
section .data      ; Section for data
    num1 db 5      ; Define byte (db) num1 with the
value 5
    num2 db 10     ; Define byte (db) num2 with the
value 10

section .bss       ; Section for uninitialized data
(if needed)

section .text      ; Section for code
```

```
    global _start    ; Tell the assembler where to
start execution

_start:
    ; Load the value of num1 into register AL
    mov al, [num1]

    ; Add the value of num2 to register AL
    add al, [num2]

    ; The result is now in AL (which is the lower 8
bits of the AX register)

    ; For simplicity, we will end the program here
    mov ah, 0x4C    ; 0x4C is the exit system call
number in DOS
    int 0x21         ; Call the DOS interrupt to exit
the program
```

Explanation of the Code:

- **section .data**: This is where we define the data section. We define two bytes (num1 and num2) and initialize them with the values 5 and 10, respectively.
- **section .text**: The code section begins here. This is where the actual operations take place.
- **mov al, [num1]**: This instruction loads the value of num1 (5) into the AL register.
- **add al, [num2]**: This instruction adds the value of num2 (10) to the AL register, which currently contains 5. After this operation, AL will contain 15.
- **mov ah, 0x4C**: The mov instruction places the system call number for exit (0x4C) into the AH register.
- **int 0x21**: This instruction triggers the DOS interrupt to exit the program.

Conclusion

In this chapter, we've explored the basics of **Assembly language**, from the human-readable mnemonics that replace machine code to the essential instructions like MOV, ADD, and JMP. We've also learned how assembly interacts with a computer's **registers** and **memory**, and how assembly provides the programmer with direct control over the CPU. Finally, through a simple program, we saw how these building blocks come together to perform a task—in this case, adding two numbers.

Assembly language is not just a tool for controlling hardware; it's a powerful language that enables developers to fine-tune performance and develop software with precise control over the system. While it can be challenging at first, understanding assembly opens the door to a deeper comprehension of how computers work at the lowest levels. As you progress in your understanding of assembly, you'll gain the ability to write efficient, high-performance code that operates directly on the hardware, giving you a unique and valuable skill set in the world of programming.

CHAPTER 4: THE CPU ARCHITECTURE AND HOW ASSEMBLY INTERACTS WITH IT

CPU Fundamentals: How the CPU Fetches, Decodes, and Executes Instructions

The CPU (Central Processing Unit) is the core component of any computing system, responsible for executing instructions that make up a program. At its heart, the CPU is designed to process data and manage the flow of operations within the system. Understanding how the CPU works is essential for any developer, particularly when working with low-level languages like Assembly, which allow direct manipulation of the CPU's resources.

1. Fetch-Decode-Execute Cycle (FDE Cycle)

The most fundamental aspect of a CPU's operation is the **fetch-decode-execute (FDE) cycle**. This cycle is a continuous loop that enables the CPU to process instructions one after another. Here's how it workss

FETCH

In the first phase, the CPU fetches an instruction from memory. The address of the instruction to be fetched is stored in a special register known as the **Program Counter (PC)**. The PC keeps track of the location of the next instruction in the sequence. Once the instruction is fetched from memory, the PC is updated to point to the next instruction.

DECODE

After the instruction is fetched, the CPU decodes it. This means that the instruction is analyzed by the **Control Unit (CU)** to understand what operation it represents. The instruction might tell the CPU to perform an arithmetic operation, access memory, jump to another part of the program, or interact with input/output devices.

The CPU decodes the instruction by breaking it down into components, such as the **opcode** (the operation to perform) and the **operand** (the data or address to use). The opcode is typically a set of bits that represent an operation, such as addition, subtraction, or data movement.

EXECUTE

Once the instruction is decoded, the CPU performs the corresponding operation. For example, if the instruction is an arithmetic operation, the **Arithmetic Logic Unit (ALU)** performs the calculation. If the instruction involves memory access, the **Memory Management Unit (MMU)** is responsible for reading or writing data to memory.

After execution, the CPU checks if the instruction affects any flags (special bits in registers that represent conditions like zero or carry) and updates them accordingly. The CPU then proceeds to the next instruction, starting the cycle again.

2. The Key Components of the CPU

To fully understand how the CPU operates, it's important to know the key components involved in executing an instruction:

A. REGISTERS

Registers are small, fast storage locations within the CPU. They hold data that is actively being processed. Registers are essential for efficient execution because they allow the CPU to access data much faster than it can from main memory. There are several types of registers:

- **General-Purpose Registers**: These registers are used to store data that is being manipulated. For example, the **AX**, **BX**, **CX**, and **DX** registers are commonly used in x86 assembly to hold intermediate values during calculations.
- **Special-Purpose Registers**: These registers serve specific functions, such as the **Program Counter (PC)**, which keeps track of the address of the next instruction to be executed, and the **Stack Pointer (SP)**, which points to the top of the stack.
- **Status Registers**: The **Flags Register** holds status bits that indicate the result of an operation. For example, if a subtraction results in zero, the Zero Flag (ZF) is set.

B. CONTROL UNIT (CU)

The Control Unit (CU) is responsible for managing and directing the execution of instructions. It interprets the decoded instruction and sends signals to other components of the CPU to carry out the specified operation. The CU also coordinates the flow of data between the CPU and memory.

C. ARITHMETIC LOGIC UNIT (ALU)

The ALU is responsible for performing arithmetic and logical operations. It carries out operations like addition, subtraction, AND, OR, and comparison. The ALU works closely with the registers to fetch the data needed for computations and store the results.

D. MEMORY MANAGEMENT UNIT (MMU)

The MMU is responsible for managing the system's memory. It handles tasks such as converting virtual memory addresses to physical memory addresses and ensuring that memory access is valid. When the CPU needs to read from or write to memory, the MMU ensures that the correct memory location is accessed.

Memory and Register Management: Using Assembly to Access and Manage Memory

Memory and registers are the two primary forms of data storage within a system, and assembly language provides powerful tools for managing them. While registers are the fastest form of storage, they are limited in number, so the CPU must rely on memory (RAM) for larger data sets.

1. Memory Addressing in Assembly

In assembly language, managing memory is a critical part of writing efficient code. There are several ways to access memory in assembly, depending on the processor architecture and the instruction set being used. Let's look at some common memory addressing modes in assembly language:

A. DIRECT ADDRESSING

Direct addressing is the simplest form of memory access, where an instruction directly specifies the memory address from which to read or write data. For example:

assembly

```
MOV AX, [1000h]   ; Move the value at memory address
1000h into register AX
```

In this case, the value stored at memory address 0x1000 is moved into the AX register.

B. INDIRECT ADDRESSING

Indirect addressing uses a register to store the address of the data in memory. For example, if the register BX contains the address 0x1000, the instruction can access the value at that address:

assembly

```
MOV AX, [BX]      ; Move the value at the memory
address stored in BX into AX
```

Indirect addressing allows for more flexible memory access and is commonly used in loops and data structures like arrays.

C. INDEXED ADDRESSING

Indexed addressing is used to access elements in an array or data structure. In this mode, the address of the data is calculated by adding a base address to an offset (or index). For example:

assembly

```
MOV AX, [BX + SI]  ; Move the value at the address
(BX + SI) into AX
```

In this example, BX might be the base address of an array, and SI is the index. This form of addressing is common in operations that involve arrays or buffers.

D. BASE REGISTER ADDRESSING

In base register addressing, the effective address is obtained by adding a constant value to the contents of a register. This is commonly used when working with data structures where the base address is stored in a register, and offsets are applied to access specific elements:

assembly

```
MOV AX, [BX + 4]  ; Move the value at the address (BX
+ 4) into AX
```

Here, the value at BX + 4 is accessed, which might be used to access the second element in a data structure.

2. Memory Management in Assembly

In assembly, you can allocate and deallocate memory dynamically, which is especially important when working with data that may change in size during program execution. For example, in some systems, the stack is used to dynamically allocate memory for function calls and local variables.

A. STACK MANAGEMENT

The stack is a special region of memory that follows the Last In, First Out (LIFO) principle. The CPU uses the **Stack Pointer (SP)** register to keep track of the top of the stack. When data is pushed onto the stack, the SP register is decremented, and when data is popped off the stack, the SP register is incremented.

Here's an example of using the stack in assembly:

```assembly
PUSH AX          ; Push the contents of AX onto the
stack
POP BX           ; Pop the top value from the stack
into BX
```

The stack is essential for managing function calls, where local variables and return addresses are stored.

Instruction Set Architectures (ISA): A Look at Different ISAs (e.g., x86, ARM)

An **Instruction Set Architecture (ISA)** defines the set of instructions that a CPU can understand and execute. It is a crucial part of a computer's hardware, as it dictates the operations that can be performed and how they are encoded in machine code. Different

CPUs have different ISAs, which is why code written for one CPU architecture might not work on another.

1. x86 Architecture

The **x86** architecture is one of the most widely used ISAs in personal computers and servers. Originally developed by Intel in the late 1970s, x86 processors are commonly found in desktops, laptops, and servers. x86 is a **CISC (Complex Instruction Set Computing)** architecture, meaning it has a large set of instructions that can perform complex operations in a single instruction.

- **Registers**: The x86 architecture has general-purpose registers such as AX, BX, CX, and DX. These registers can hold data, addresses, and intermediate results during program execution.
- **Addressing Modes**: x86 supports several addressing modes, including direct, indirect, and indexed addressing.
- **Instruction Set**: The x86 instruction set includes a broad range of instructions for data movement, arithmetic, logic, and control flow, making it a versatile ISA.

2. ARM Architecture

ARM (Advanced RISC Machines) is a different type of ISA that follows the **RISC (Reduced Instruction Set Computing)** philosophy. RISC architectures focus on simplicity and efficiency by using a smaller, more streamlined set of instructions that can execute faster.

ARM processors are widely used in mobile devices like smartphones, tablets, and embedded systems due to their power efficiency. ARM also has a much more simplified instruction set compared to x86, which can result in better performance for certain applications.

- **Registers**: ARM has a set of general-purpose registers, along with special-purpose registers such as the **Program Counter (PC)** and **Status Register (CPSR)**.
- **Addressing Modes**: ARM supports several addressing modes like register, immediate, and offset addressing, enabling flexible memory access.
- **Instruction Set**: ARM's instruction set is smaller but highly efficient, emphasizing simplicity and speed.

3. Other ISAs

There are several other ISAs used in specific applications, such as **MIPS**, **SPARC**, and **PowerPC**. Each has its unique characteristics and use cases, but they all share the same basic principles of instruction encoding, execution, and memory management.

Hands-on Example: Writing a Simple Assembly Program That Accesses and Modifies Memory

Now that we have a solid understanding of CPU architecture, memory management, and ISAs, let's put these concepts into practice by writing a simple assembly program that accesses and modifies memory.

Program Objective

This program will demonstrate how to:

- Access data stored in memory.
- Modify the data.

- Store the modified data back into memory.

Example Program (x86 Assembly)

```assembly
assembly

section .data
    num1 db 5              ; Define a byte with the
value 5
    num2 db 10             ; Define another byte with
the value 10

section .text
    global _start

_start:
    ; Load the value of num1 into register AL
    mov al, [num1]

    ; Add the value of num2 to the value in AL
    add al, [num2]

    ; Store the result back into num1
    mov [num1], al

    ; Exit the program
    mov eax, 1            ; System call number for
exit
    xor ebx, ebx         ; Return code 0
    int 0x80             ; Interrupt to exit the
program
```

Explanation of the Code:

1. **Data Section**: We define two variables (num1 and num2) in the .data section of memory. Each is initialized with a value (5 and 10).
2. **Text Section**: This is where the executable code goes.
   o We first load the value stored in num1 into the AL register.

- Then, we add the value stored in `num2` to `AL`.
- The result is stored back into the `num1` location in memory.
3. **Program Exit**: The program exits cleanly by calling the `exit` system call (`int 0x80`).

Conclusion

In this chapter, we explored the fundamentals of the CPU, including the fetch-decode-execute cycle, and how the CPU processes instructions. We also learned about memory and register management, with a focus on how assembly language allows us to interact with the CPU's registers and memory. We also reviewed different instruction set architectures (ISAs) like x86 and ARM, and how each defines the capabilities of a CPU.

By understanding the CPU architecture and how assembly interacts with it, developers can gain a deeper insight into how programs execute at the hardware level. This knowledge is invaluable for optimizing performance, debugging low-level code, and working with systems that require fine-grained control over hardware resources. The hands-on examples provided in this chapter offer a practical foundation for working with assembly, and as you continue to learn, you'll gain more confidence in managing memory, registers, and low-level instructions effectively.

CHAPTER 5: THE ROLE OF THE OPERATING SYSTEM IN LOW-LEVEL PROGRAMMING

System Calls and Interrupts: How the Operating System Interfaces with Low-Level Code

In low-level programming, the operating system (OS) plays a crucial role by managing hardware resources, handling communication between software and hardware, and ensuring the smooth execution of processes. Low-level programming languages, such as Assembly, allow for direct interaction with hardware, but this interaction is often mediated by the operating system. The OS provides a structured interface for programs to request services, access system resources, and communicate with external devices through system calls and interrupts.

1. What Are System Calls?

A **system call** is a mechanism that allows user programs to request services from the operating system's kernel. The operating system provides a set of predefined system calls that programs can use to perform tasks that require privileged access to hardware or system resources, such as reading from or writing to a file, allocating memory, or creating new processes.

In high-level programming, system calls are typically abstracted by libraries or built-in functions, so programmers don't need to deal with the low-level details. However, in low-level programming, particularly with Assembly, system calls are invoked directly and can provide powerful functionality.

When a program makes a system call, it typically triggers a **software interrupt** to shift the control from user mode (where the program runs) to kernel mode (where the operating system's core code executes). Once the operating system has completed the requested task, control is returned to the program, which resumes execution.

2. How System Calls Work

A system call generally works through a process known as a **context switch**. When a program makes a system call, it passes data through registers or the stack, which is then interpreted by the kernel to determine which system service to invoke. The program then enters a special state called kernel mode, where it can safely access hardware resources.

For example, in Linux, making a system call involves placing the system call number (a unique identifier for each system call) in a specific register, along with any necessary parameters, before triggering a software interrupt. The operating system will then decode the system call, execute the corresponding kernel function, and return any results to the calling program.

Here's an example of a system call in Linux using Assembly:

```
assembly

; Example of a system call to write data to the
console
```

```
section .data
    msg db 'Hello, World!', 0x0A    ; Message to be
printed

section .text
    global _start

_start:
    ; Write system call (sys_write)
    mov eax, 4                      ; sys_write = 4
    mov ebx, 1                      ; File
descriptor: 1 (stdout)
    mov ecx, msg                    ; Address of the
message
    mov edx, 14                     ; Length of the
message
    int 0x80                        ; Interrupt to
invoke the system call

    ; Exit system call (sys_exit)
    mov eax, 1                      ; sys_exit = 1
    xor ebx, ebx                    ; Exit code 0
    int 0x80                        ; Interrupt to
invoke the system call
```

3. Interrupts: The Mechanism Behind System Calls

An **interrupt** is a signal to the CPU that requires immediate
attention. Interrupts can be generated by hardware (hardware
interrupts) or software (software interrupts). When an interrupt
occurs, the CPU stops executing the current instructions, saves its
state, and jumps to a special routine to handle the interrupt. After
the interrupt is serviced, the CPU returns to the point where it left
off.

System calls are often implemented using software interrupts,
where a program generates an interrupt to switch from user mode to
kernel mode. For example, in the Linux operating system, the `int`
`0x80` instruction is used to trigger a system call interrupt.

4. Types of System Calls

System calls fall into several categories, each serving a different purpose. Some common types include:

- **Process Control**: These system calls handle tasks such as creating, scheduling, and terminating processes. Examples include `fork` (create a new process) and `exit` (terminate a process).
- **File Management**: System calls in this category allow programs to create, read, write, and manipulate files. Examples include `open`, `read`, `write`, and `close`.
- **Memory Management**: These system calls manage the allocation and deallocation of memory for processes. Examples include `malloc` (allocate memory) and `free` (deallocate memory).
- **Device Management**: These system calls provide access to hardware devices like disk drives and network interfaces. Examples include `ioctl` (device control) and `read`/`write` for I/O operations.
- **Communication**: System calls that allow processes to communicate with each other, such as `pipe`, `socket`, and `mmap`.

Memory Management: How OS Allocates Memory for Processes

The operating system is responsible for managing memory resources efficiently, ensuring that each process has access to the memory it needs while preventing conflicts between processes. Memory management is a critical function of the OS, as it directly impacts the performance, stability, and security of the system.

1. Virtual Memory: Abstraction of Physical Memory

Most modern operating systems implement **virtual memory**, which abstracts the physical memory of the computer and provides each process with the illusion of having its own dedicated address space. Virtual memory allows the OS to use techniques like **paging** and **segmentation** to map virtual memory addresses to physical memory locations.

The operating system uses the **Memory Management Unit (MMU)** to perform the mapping between virtual and physical memory. The MMU translates virtual memory addresses into physical addresses, ensuring that processes do not interfere with each other's memory.

2. Memory Allocation: The Role of System Calls

When a program requests memory, it typically uses system calls to allocate or deallocate memory. For example, in Unix-like operating systems, a process might use the `mmap` system call to allocate memory, or `brk` to set the program break (the end of the heap). These system calls request memory from the OS, which then provides a block of virtual memory.

The OS keeps track of memory allocation using data structures like **page tables**, which store the mapping between virtual memory addresses and physical memory. When a program accesses a memory address, the OS checks the page table to determine if the virtual address is mapped to a valid physical address.

3. Memory Protection and Segmentation

The operating system also implements **memory protection** to prevent one process from accessing another process's memory.

This is done by assigning **access rights** to each page of memory, such as read, write, and execute permissions. The OS uses these rights to enforce isolation between processes, ensuring that one process cannot corrupt or steal data from another.

Segmentation is another technique used to manage memory. In segmentation, the memory is divided into different segments, such as the code segment, data segment, stack, and heap. Each segment has a different purpose, and the OS ensures that programs use these segments correctly. For example, the stack is used for function calls and local variables, while the heap is used for dynamic memory allocation.

Context Switching: How the OS Handles Multitasking

Context switching is the process by which the operating system manages multitasking. Since modern CPUs can only execute one instruction at a time, the operating system allows multiple processes to run concurrently by rapidly switching between them. This creates the illusion of parallel execution, even on single-core processors.

1. The Need for Context Switching

Context switching occurs when the CPU switches from executing one process to executing another. This is necessary for multitasking, where the OS gives each process a share of the CPU's time. In a preemptive multitasking system, the OS decides when a process should be paused and when another process should be executed.

For example, if process A is running and needs to wait for I/O, the OS may switch to process B, which is ready to execute. This ensures that the CPU remains busy and that all processes get a fair share of CPU time.

2. The Context Switch Process

Context switching involves saving the state of the currently running process and restoring the state of the next process to run. The **context** of a process includes the values of its registers, program counter, and stack pointer. When the OS decides to switch processes, it performs the following steps:

1. **Save the State**: The OS saves the current state of the process (its registers, program counter, and other information) to a **process control block (PCB)** or a similar data structure.
2. **Select the Next Process**: The OS selects the next process to run based on its scheduling algorithm. The scheduler chooses the process that is ready to run, such as one that has completed its I/O operation or has a higher priority.
3. **Restore the State**: The OS restores the state of the selected process from its PCB. This includes loading the saved values of its registers and program counter, so the process can resume from where it left off.
4. **Update the Process Control Block**: The OS updates the PCB to reflect the new state of the process, including whether it is running, waiting, or blocked.

3. The Role of System Calls in Context Switching

Context switching relies heavily on system calls to save and restore the state of processes. For instance, when a process makes a system call that involves waiting for I/O, the operating system may need to suspend the process and allow another process to run. The OS will save the state of the suspended process and schedule another process to execute in its place.

System calls like `sleep`, `wait`, and `yield` are often used to trigger context switching, as they allow a process to voluntarily relinquish control of the CPU, either because it is waiting for an event or because it has completed its task.

Hands-on Example: Writing a Program to Interact with the OS Through System Calls

In this section, we will write a simple assembly program that interacts with the operating system by using system calls to read input, process data, and print output.

Example: Simple Input/Output Program Using Linux System Calls

```assembly
section .data
    prompt db 'Enter a number: ', 0
    result db 'The number is: ', 0

section .bss
    num resb 4              ; Reserve space for 4 bytes
(int)

section .text
    global _start

_start:
    ; Display the prompt message
```

```
        mov eax, 4            ; sys_write
        mov ebx, 1            ; file descriptor 1 (stdout)
        mov ecx, prompt       ; address of the prompt
message
        mov edx, 16           ; length of the prompt
message
        int 0x80              ; call the kernel

        ; Read user input (number)
        mov eax, 3            ; sys_read
        mov ebx, 0            ; file descriptor 0 (stdin)
        mov ecx, num          ; buffer to store input
        mov edx, 4            ; number of bytes to read
        int 0x80              ; call the kernel

        ; Display the result message
        mov eax, 4            ; sys_write
        mov ebx, 1            ; file descriptor 1 (stdout)
        mov ecx, result       ; address of the result
message
        mov edx, 16           ; length of the result
message
        int 0x80              ; call the kernel

        ; Display the entered number (this would need to
be converted from string to int in real applications)
        mov eax, 4            ; sys_write
        mov ebx, 1            ; file descriptor 1 (stdout)
        mov ecx, num          ; address of the input
number
        mov edx, 4            ; number of bytes to write
        int 0x80              ; call the kernel

        ; Exit the program
        mov eax, 1            ; sys_exit
        xor ebx, ebx          ; exit code 0
        int 0x80              ; call the kernel
```

Explanation of the Code:

1. **Prompting the User**: The program begins by displaying a prompt asking the user to enter a number using the `sys_write` system call.
2. **Reading Input**: The program then uses the `sys_read` system call to read the user's input from the terminal (stdin) into a buffer.
3. **Displaying the Result**: The program uses `sys_write` again to display a message indicating that it will print the entered number.
4. **Exiting**: Finally, the program exits using the `sys_exit` system call.

This program demonstrates how assembly language can directly interact with the operating system through system calls to perform basic input/output operations.

Conclusion

This chapter has explored the crucial role of the operating system in low-level programming, focusing on how system calls, interrupts, memory management, and context switching all contribute to managing resources and executing processes. By understanding the relationship between assembly code and the operating system, programmers can write more efficient and powerful low-level programs that make the most of the underlying hardware and system resources. The hands-on examples provided illustrate how to interact with the OS through system calls and how low-level programming interfaces with the OS to accomplish common tasks.

CHAPTER 6: ADVANCED ASSEMBLY LANGUAGE TECHNIQUES

Introduction

In the world of low-level programming, **Assembly Language** is both powerful and intricate. Mastering the basic instructions like MOV, ADD, and JMP is only the first step; as developers progress, they must explore more advanced techniques to write efficient, reusable, and optimized code. In this chapter, we will dive into advanced topics that allow you to fully harness the power of Assembly. We will explore **macros and loops**, **stack and heap management**, and **optimization techniques** that help you write faster, smaller, and more maintainable assembly code.

1. Macros and Loops in Assembly: Writing Reusable Code in Assembly

One of the limitations of Assembly is that, by default, every instruction is written manually. This can lead to repetitive code, which is not only cumbersome to write but also prone to errors. Fortunately, **macros** and **loops** offer ways to make your code more reusable and efficient.

1.1 What Are Macros?

A **macro** is a set of instructions that are grouped together under a single name. Instead of writing the same sequence of instructions multiple times throughout your code, you can define a macro once and then invoke it whenever needed. Macros can take parameters, allowing for more flexible and reusable code.

Macros in assembly work like templates. When you invoke a macro, the assembler expands the macro definition and inserts the corresponding instructions in place of the macro call. This avoids the redundancy of writing the same code over and over, especially in large programs.

Let's look at an example of a simple macro in assembly:

```assembly
%macro PRINT_MSG 2
    mov eax, 4          ; sys_write system call
    mov ebx, 1          ; file descriptor (stdout)
    mov ecx, %1         ; address of the string
    mov edx, %2         ; length of the string
    int 0x80            ; call the kernel
%endmacro

section .data
    msg db "Hello, world!", 0x0A
    len equ $ - msg

section .text
    global _start

_start:
    PRINT_MSG msg, len  ; Call the macro with the
message and length
    mov eax, 1          ; sys_exit
    xor ebx, ebx        ; exit code 0
    int 0x80            ; call the kernel
```

In this example, the PRINT_MSG macro is defined to print a message to the screen. The macro takes two parameters: the address of the message and the length of the message. By calling PRINT_MSG in the code, the assembler will expand it into the corresponding instructions. This makes the code more readable and maintainable.

1.2 Loops in Assembly

A **loop** is a fundamental programming structure that allows you to repeat a set of instructions multiple times. In Assembly, loops can be implemented with a combination of jump instructions (JMP, JE, JNE, etc.) and conditional checks.

Here's an example of how a simple loop works in Assembly:

```assembly
section .data
    msg db "Counting from 1 to 5:", 0x0A
    len equ $ - msg

section .bss
    count resb 1                ; Reserve 1 byte for the
counter

section .text
    global _start

_start:
    ; Print the initial message
    mov eax, 4
    mov ebx, 1
    mov ecx, msg
    mov edx, len
    int 0x80

    ; Initialize counter to 1
    mov byte [count], 1

loop_start:
    ; Print the current counter value
    mov al, [count]
```

```
    ; (Printing logic would go here, omitted for
brevity)

    ; Increment the counter
    inc byte [count]

    ; Check if the counter has reached 6
    cmp byte [count], 6
    jl loop_start          ; Jump back to loop_start
if count < 6

    ; Exit the program
    mov eax, 1
    xor ebx, ebx
    int 0x80
```

In this example, the counter starts at 1 and is incremented in each iteration of the loop. The CMP instruction compares the counter with 6, and the JL instruction causes the loop to continue as long as the counter is less than 6. This is a basic example of a loop in Assembly.

2. Stack and Heap Management: Handling Memory Dynamically in Assembly

Memory management is one of the most complex aspects of low-level programming. In high-level languages, memory allocation is usually handled automatically by the system or runtime environment. However, in Assembly, developers must take direct control of memory management.

There are two main types of memory used in most programs: the **stack** and the **heap**.

2.1 The Stack:

The **stack** is a region of memory used for storing temporary data, such as function arguments, local variables, and return addresses. It operates on a **Last In, First Out (LIFO)** principle, where the most recently pushed item is the first to be popped off the stack.

In Assembly, you interact with the stack using **push** and **pop** instructions:

- **PUSH**: Adds an item to the stack.
- **POP**: Removes the most recent item from the stack.

Here's an example of using the stack to store and retrieve data:

```assembly
section .data
    msg db "Stack example", 0x0A
    len equ $ - msg

section .text
    global _start

_start:
    ; Push data onto the stack
    mov eax, 5
    push eax                ; Push the value 5 onto the stack
    mov eax, 10
    push eax                ; Push the value 10 onto the stack

    ; Pop data from the stack
    pop ebx                 ; Pop the top value (10) into ebx
    pop eax                 ; Pop the next value (5) into eax

    ; Print the message
```

```
mov eax, 4
mov ebx, 1
mov ecx, msg
mov edx, len
int 0x80

; Exit the program
mov eax, 1
xor ebx, ebx
int 0x80
```

In this example, we push two values (5 and 10) onto the stack and then pop them back into registers (`eax` and `ebx`).

2.2 The Heap:

The **heap** is used for dynamic memory allocation. Unlike the stack, the heap is managed manually by the programmer and does not follow a LIFO structure. The OS is responsible for managing the heap and allocating memory to processes as needed.

In Assembly, memory allocation on the heap can be done using system calls, such as `mmap` or `brk` on Linux. These system calls allow programs to request memory from the OS dynamically.

Here's an example of how you might allocate memory using the `mmap` system call in Linux (this is a simplified version):

```
assembly

section .data
    size equ 4096          ; Size of memory to allocate
(4KB)

section .text
    global _start

_start:
```

```asm
; Allocate memory using mmap (system call 90)
mov eax, 90          ; sys_mmap = 90
xor ebx, ebx         ; addr = 0 (auto-allocate)
mov ecx, size        ; length = size
xor edx, edx         ; protection = PROT_READ |
PROT_WRITE
xor esi, esi         ; flags = MAP_PRIVATE |
MAP_ANONYMOUS
xor edi, edi         ; fd = -1 (not using a file)
xor ebp, ebp         ; offset = 0
int 0x80             ; Call the kernel

; Check for successful allocation
; If the return value is negative, the allocation
failed

; Exit the program
mov eax, 1           ; sys_exit
xor ebx, ebx         ; exit code 0
int 0x80
```

In this example, we use the mmap system call to allocate 4KB of memory. The memory is mapped into the process's address space and can be used dynamically during execution.

---

3. Optimizing Assembly Code: Techniques to Write Efficient and Compact Assembly Code

One of the main advantages of Assembly is the ability to write highly optimized code. However, it's not enough to simply write functional code—**efficiency** and **compactness** are crucial, especially in resource-constrained environments like embedded systems.

3.1 Reducing Instruction Count

One of the main ways to optimize Assembly code is to reduce the number of instructions. Each instruction takes time to execute, so minimizing the total number of instructions can improve performance. Some techniques include:

- **Combining operations**: Instead of writing separate instructions for related operations, try to combine them into fewer steps.

  Example:

  assembly

  ```
  ; Less efficient
  mov eax, 5
  add eax, 10
  mov ebx, eax

  ; More efficient
  add eax, 10    ; Directly adding without using
  extra registers
  ```

- **Using more powerful instructions**: Some CPU instructions are more complex and can perform multiple operations in a single instruction. For example, the LEA (Load Effective Address) instruction can perform address calculations in a single step, avoiding the need for multiple MOV or ADD operations.

3.2 Minimizing Memory Access

Memory access is much slower than register access. To improve performance, it's crucial to minimize the number of memory accesses. You can do this by:

- **Using registers as temporary storage**: Whenever possible, perform calculations in registers instead of frequently accessing memory.

  Example:

  ```assembly
  ; Instead of
  mov eax, [var1]
  add eax, [var2]
  mov [result], eax

  ; Do this
  mov eax, [var1]
  add eax, [var2]
  mov [result], eax
  ```

- **Caching values**: If you need to use the same value multiple times, load it into a register and use it from there rather than repeatedly accessing memory.

3.3 Using Efficient Branching

Branching operations like JMP (jump) and CALL (function call) can be costly if used excessively. To optimize your code:

- **Minimize the number of conditional branches**: Use loops and conditional jumps efficiently to avoid unnecessary branching.
- **Unrolling loops**: Loop unrolling is a technique where the body of a loop is duplicated multiple times in the code, thus reducing the overhead of the loop control.

Example of loop unrolling:

```
assembly

; Original loop
mov ecx, 10
loop_start:
    ; Do something
    dec ecx
    jnz loop_start

; Unrolled loop
mov eax, 10
; First iteration
    ; Do something
; Second iteration
    ; Do something
; etc.
```

3.4 Reducing Instruction Size

Another important factor in optimization is **instruction size**. The fewer bits each instruction takes, the more compact the program will be. To achieve this, you should:

- **Use 8-bit registers** where possible: Many CPUs support 32-bit or even 64-bit registers, but for simple tasks, 8-bit registers might be sufficient and require less space.
- **Optimize data storage**: Store data types efficiently. For example, use `byte` instead of `word` when you only need a small range of values.

4. Hands-on Example: Optimizing a Sorting Algorithm Using Assembly

Now that we've explored the techniques for optimization, let's put them to use by optimizing a **sorting algorithm** in Assembly. Sorting is a basic algorithm, but optimizing it in Assembly can provide a significant boost in performance, especially for large datasets.

We'll implement **Bubble Sort**, a simple yet inefficient algorithm, and then optimize it.

4.1 Basic Bubble Sort

Here's a simple implementation of Bubble Sort in Assembly (using x86 syntax):

```assembly
section .data
    arr db 5, 2, 9, 1, 5, 6
    len equ 6

section .text
    global _start

_start:
    mov ecx, len        ; Outer loop counter (number
of passes)
outer_loop:
    mov ebx, 0          ; Inner loop counter
    mov edx, 0          ; Flag to check if a swap
occurred

inner_loop:
    ; Compare adjacent elements
    mov al, [arr + ebx]
    mov ah, [arr + ebx + 1]
    cmp al, ah
    jg swap_elements

    ; If no swap, continue to the next pair
    inc ebx
    loop inner_loop
    dec ecx
    jnz outer_loop
```

```asm
    jmp done

swap_elements:
    ; Swap the elements
    mov al, [arr + ebx]
    mov ah, [arr + ebx + 1]
    mov [arr + ebx], ah
    mov [arr + ebx + 1], al

    ; Set flag to indicate a swap occurred
    mov edx, 1
    inc ebx
    loop inner_loop
    dec ecx
    jnz outer_loop

done:
    ; Exit the program
    mov eax, 1              ; sys_exit
    xor ebx, ebx           ; exit code 0
    int 0x80               ; call the kernel
```

This basic implementation compares adjacent elements and swaps them if needed. The outer loop runs until no swaps occur during a full pass through the array.

4.2 Optimized Bubble Sort

We can optimize this algorithm by reducing the number of passes. If no elements were swapped during the inner loop, we can conclude that the array is already sorted and exit early.

```asm
assembly

section .data
    arr db 5, 2, 9, 1, 5, 6
    len equ 6

section .text
    global _start
```

```
_start:
    mov ecx, len          ; Outer loop counter (number
of passes)
outer_loop:
    mov ebx, 0            ; Inner loop counter
    mov edx, 0            ; Flag to check if a swap
occurred

inner_loop:
    ; Compare adjacent elements
    mov al, [arr + ebx]
    mov ah, [arr + ebx + 1]
    cmp al, ah
    jg swap_elements

    ; If no swap, continue to the next pair
    inc ebx
    loop inner_loop

    ; If no swaps occurred, exit early
    cmp edx, 0
    je done
    dec ecx
    jnz outer_loop

swap_elements:
    ; Swap the elements
    mov al, [arr + ebx]
    mov ah, [arr + ebx + 1]
    mov [arr + ebx], ah
    mov [arr + ebx + 1], al

    ; Set flag to indicate a swap occurred
    mov edx, 1
    inc ebx
    loop inner_loop
    dec ecx
    jnz outer_loop

done:
    ; Exit the program
    mov eax, 1            ; sys_exit
    xor ebx, ebx          ; exit code 0
```

```
int 0x80                    ; call the kernel
```

In this optimized version, the program keeps track of whether any swaps occurred during the inner loop. If no swaps occur, the program exits early, significantly reducing the number of unnecessary passes.

Conclusion

In this chapter, we've covered **advanced assembly language techniques** to help you write more efficient, maintainable, and reusable code. We've explored the concept of **macros** for reusable code, **loops** for repeating tasks efficiently, and memory management with the **stack** and **heap**. We also discussed how to optimize assembly code by reducing instruction count, minimizing memory access, and using efficient branching.

Through the hands-on examples, we've seen how to implement and optimize a sorting algorithm, demonstrating how low-level techniques can be applied to solve real-world problems. With these techniques in your toolkit, you'll be able to write faster, smaller, and more optimized assembly programs, taking full advantage of the power of low-level programming.

CHAPTER 7: DEBUGGING AND TROUBLESHOOTING LOW-LEVEL CODE

Introduction

In low-level programming, especially with Assembly, bugs can be elusive and difficult to track down. Unlike high-level programming languages that offer robust debugging tools and error handling mechanisms, Assembly operates closer to the hardware, offering less abstraction but greater control. This makes debugging a critical skill for any assembly programmer. In this chapter, we will dive into common bugs found in assembly programs, explore debugging tools like **GDB** (GNU Debugger), and discuss how to use stack traces and core dumps to analyze and resolve runtime errors. We will also walk through a hands-on debugging example to demonstrate how to troubleshoot assembly code using GDB.

1. Common Bugs in Assembly

Low-level programming in Assembly exposes the programmer directly to the machine's architecture, which means the range of errors can vary significantly. Some bugs are easy to identify, while others can be challenging because they involve issues such as incorrect memory access, misalignment, or improper use of registers. Let's explore some of the most common bugs in Assembly language.

1.1 Syntax Errors

Syntax errors are the most basic type of bug and occur when the assembly code does not conform to the rules of the assembly language syntax. These errors typically result in the assembler failing to assemble the code into machine code.

Example of a syntax error:

assembly

```
MOV AX, [1000h] ; Correct syntax for loading a value
from memory
MOV [1000h], AX ; Missing square brackets around AX
```

In the second line, the absence of square brackets around AX would be a syntax error, as the assembler would interpret it as a literal value instead of a register.

1.2 Undefined or Uninitialized Registers

Assembly programming requires careful management of registers. Using uninitialized or undefined registers in operations can cause unexpected behavior and bugs that may be difficult to identify. If a register is not properly initialized before use, it could contain garbage values that lead to incorrect program behavior.

Example:

assembly

```
MOV AX, 10    ; Initialize AX with 10
ADD BX, AX    ; Add AX to BX (but BX is uninitialized)
```

In this case, BX is uninitialized, and the result of BX + AX is unpredictable.

1.3 Incorrect Memory Access

Accessing memory incorrectly is a frequent issue in Assembly. Whether it's using the wrong addressing mode, referencing memory outside the allocated bounds, or reading/writing to the wrong address, improper memory access can lead to program crashes or data corruption.

Example:

```assembly
MOV AX, [0x1000]    ; Correctly reading from memory
address 0x1000
MOV [0x2000], AX    ; Correctly writing to memory
address 0x2000
MOV AX, [0x3000]    ; Attempting to read from an
unallocated or protected address
```

Reading from an unallocated or protected memory address can cause segmentation faults or memory access violations.

1.4 Stack Overflow

A **stack overflow** occurs when a program uses more stack space than is allocated. In Assembly, this often happens when there are too many function calls or too many local variables, leading to the stack growing beyond its allocated bounds.

Example:

```assembly
PUSH EAX        ; Pushing values onto the stack
without managing stack space properly
PUSH EBX
```

```
; Continually pushing values without balancing with
POP instructions
```

When a function repeatedly calls itself or the stack is not managed correctly, the system can run out of space for function calls, leading to a stack overflow.

1.5 Off-by-One Errors

An **off-by-one error** happens when the program reads or writes one byte or word too much or too little. This type of error can be especially problematic when dealing with buffers or arrays, as it can lead to corrupted data or memory access violations.

Example:

```
assembly

MOV CX, 5          ; Loop counter (for an array of 5
elements)
MOV SI, 0          ; Array index (starting at 0)
loop_start:
    MOV AX, [array + SI]    ; Reading an element from
the array
    INC SI
    LOOP loop_start
```

In this case, the loop will run 6 times instead of 5 because the initial value of SI should be incremented after accessing the array. The last iteration will access memory outside the bounds of the array, leading to potential corruption or crashes.

2. Using Debuggers: Tools like GDB for Debugging Assembly Programs

Debugging assembly code can be tricky without the right tools. **GDB** (GNU Debugger) is one of the most powerful debugging tools available for assembly and C programs. It allows you to step through code, inspect the values in registers and memory, and track down bugs systematically. Below, we'll explore how to use GDB for debugging assembly programs.

2.1 Setting Up GDB

Before using GDB, you need to ensure that your assembly program is compiled with debugging symbols. Debugging symbols allow GDB to map machine code instructions back to their corresponding lines in the source code.

For example, to assemble and link an assembly program with debugging symbols:

```bash
nasm -f elf64 -g -F dwarf program.asm    # Assemble
with debug info
ld -o program program.o                   # Link the
object file
```

The `-g` flag in `nasm` generates debug information, and the `-F dwarf` option specifies the debug format.

2.2 Basic GDB Commands

Once you've compiled your program with debug symbols, you can start GDB to debug your program:

```bash
gdb ./program
```

Here are some basic GDB commands that are useful for debugging assembly programs:

- **run**: Starts the program within GDB.
- **break <line number>**: Sets a breakpoint at a specific line in the code. For example, `break 20` sets a breakpoint at line 20.
- **step**: Executes the next instruction, stepping into function calls if there are any.
- **next**: Executes the next instruction but steps over function calls (does not enter the function).
- **continue**: Resumes execution after a breakpoint has been hit.
- **info registers**: Displays the values in all CPU registers.
- **x/10xw <memory address>**: Examines memory. For example, `x/10xw 0x1000` will display 10 words of memory starting from address `0x1000`.

2.3 Setting Breakpoints and Stepping Through Code

One of the most powerful features of GDB is the ability to set breakpoints and step through the code. A breakpoint halts execution at a specified line, allowing you to inspect the state of the program.

For example, suppose you have the following assembly code:

```assembly
MOV AX, [num1]    ; Load num1 into AX
ADD AX, [num2]    ; Add num2 to AX
MOV [result], AX  ; Store the result
```

You can set a breakpoint at any of the instructions to inspect the state of registers and memory:

bash

```
(gdb) break 4
(gdb) run
```

This will set a breakpoint at line 4, where MOV AX, [num1] occurs, allowing you to inspect the contents of the registers and memory before the operation is executed.

2.4 Inspecting Registers and Memory

When debugging, it's essential to monitor the values in registers and memory. Use the info registers command to display the contents of the CPU registers. You can also inspect memory using the x command:

bash

```
(gdb) info registers
(gdb) x/10xw 0x1000
```

This will print the values of the registers and display the contents of memory starting from address 0x1000.

3. Stack Traces and Core Dumps: Analyzing and Resolving Runtime Errors

When a program crashes, it's important to understand what happened. **Stack traces** and **core dumps** are essential tools for diagnosing runtime errors. These techniques allow you to see the state of the program at the moment it crashed and trace back to the source of the error.

3.1 What is a Stack Trace?

A **stack trace** is a report generated by the operating system or debugger that provides information about the function calls leading up to the crash. It shows the call stack, which includes the sequence of function calls that were active at the time of the crash.

In low-level programming, a stack trace typically includes memory addresses of function calls, the values of local variables, and the instruction pointer at the time of the crash.

To generate a stack trace, you can use GDB:

```bash
(gdb) run
(gdb) backtrace
```

The `backtrace` command in GDB shows the call stack, making it easier to pinpoint where the program failed.

3.2 Core Dumps: What Are They?

A **core dump** is a file that captures the memory state of a running program at the moment it crashes. This file contains valuable information about the state of the program's memory, registers, and stack, which can be analyzed later to debug the problem.

To enable core dumps on most systems, you can use the following command:

```bash
bash
```

```bash
ulimit -c unlimited   # Allow core dumps to be created
```

When the program crashes, the operating system will generate a core dump file (usually named `core` or `core.<pid>`). You can then use GDB to analyze the core dump:

```bash
bash
```

```
gdb ./program core
(gdb) bt
```

This loads the program and core dump into GDB, and the `bt` (backtrace) command prints the stack trace from the core dump, helping you understand the state of the program at the time of the crash.

3.3 Resolving Runtime Errors

To resolve runtime errors using stack traces and core dumps, follow these steps:

1. **Examine the Stack Trace**: Identify the function where the error occurred and trace back through the function calls. Look for issues like invalid memory access, invalid registers, or logic errors.
2. **Inspect Memory**: Use GDB to check the values of memory locations, registers, and stack variables. Make sure that the memory is properly allocated, and there are no out-of-bounds accesses.
3. **Check Function Arguments**: Ensure that the function arguments passed to each function are correct. A common source of errors in assembly programs is incorrect or uninitialized arguments.

4. **Step Through the Code**: Use GDB's stepping features to walk through the code line-by-line and monitor how the program state changes. This can help pinpoint exactly where the error occurs.

4. Hands-on Example: Debugging an Assembly Program with GDB

Let's look at a concrete example of debugging an assembly program using GDB. Suppose you have the following assembly code that attempts to divide two numbers:

```assembly
assembly

section .data
    num1 db 10
    num2 db 2
    result db 0

section .text
    global _start

_start:
    mov al, [num1]      ; Load num1 into AL
    mov bl, [num2]      ; Load num2 into BL
    div bl              ; Divide AL by BL
    mov [result], al    ; Store result in result
    mov eax, 1          ; sys_exit
    xor ebx, ebx        ; Exit code 0
    int 0x80
```

In this program, the div instruction is used to divide num1 by num2. However, if num2 is zero, this will result in a **divide-by-zero error**.

Step 1: Compile the Program

First, compile the assembly program with debugging symbols:

bash

```
nasm -f elf64 -g -F dwarf program.asm
ld -o program program.o
```

Step 2: Run the Program in GDB

Now, let's run the program in GDB:

bash

```
gdb ./program
```

Inside GDB, run the program:

bash

```
(gdb) run
```

The program will crash with a divide-by-zero error. To get more information, we use the `backtrace` command:

bash

```
(gdb) backtrace
```

This will display the call stack, which helps us identify that the error occurred at the `div` instruction. From here, we can add safeguards to check for division by zero and prevent the crash.

Conclusion

Debugging low-level code in Assembly can be challenging, but with the right tools and techniques, you can systematically identify and resolve errors. In this chapter, we covered common bugs in assembly, including syntax errors, undefined registers, memory access issues, stack overflows, and off-by-one errors. We also explored how to use debugging tools like **GDB** to set breakpoints, inspect memory and registers, and analyze stack traces and core dumps to diagnose runtime errors. With the hands-on examples provided, you now have the skills to debug assembly programs effectively and troubleshoot low-level code with confidence.

CHAPTER 8: ASSEMBLY IN EMBEDDED SYSTEMS

Introduction

Embedded systems are specialized computing systems designed to perform dedicated functions within a larger system. Unlike general-purpose computers, which are designed to run a variety of applications, embedded systems are built to perform specific tasks reliably and efficiently. These systems are pervasive in everyday life, powering everything from household appliances to automobiles, medical devices, and industrial machinery. A critical feature of many embedded systems is the need for precise, low-level control, making **Assembly language** an essential tool for embedded systems developers.

In this chapter, we will explore the role of Assembly language in embedded systems, focusing on its advantages, challenges, and techniques for real-time operation, power efficiency, and resource management. We will also provide a hands-on example of using Assembly to control an embedded system, demonstrating how Assembly can be applied in practical applications.

1. What Are Embedded Systems?

An **embedded system** is a specialized computing system that performs specific functions or tasks within a larger system. Unlike general-purpose computers, which can run multiple applications and handle complex tasks, embedded systems are optimized to perform a single or a limited set of tasks.

Embedded systems are often integrated with hardware, and they have dedicated resources such as memory, processing power, and input/output interfaces. These systems are usually designed to be efficient in terms of both processing power and energy consumption. Additionally, embedded systems often operate under tight constraints, such as real-time processing requirements, limited memory, and low power availability.

1.1 Components of Embedded Systems

An embedded system typically consists of three key components:

1. **Hardware**: This includes the microcontroller or microprocessor, memory (RAM and ROM), input/output interfaces, and any peripherals (sensors, motors, displays, etc.).
2. **Software**: This refers to the firmware or software that runs on the microcontroller to control the hardware and perform the necessary tasks. In many cases, the software is written in low-level languages like C or Assembly for efficiency.
3. **Real-Time Operating System (RTOS)**: While some embedded systems operate without an OS, others use a real-time operating system (RTOS) that guarantees predictable response times for critical tasks. An RTOS helps manage multiple tasks, ensuring they meet strict timing requirements.

1.2 Microcontrollers in Embedded Systems

Microcontrollers are the heart of most embedded systems. These small, cost-effective processors are designed to control devices and systems. They include the CPU, memory, and I/O ports on a single chip, making them ideal for embedded applications. Microcontrollers come in many varieties, such as **ARM**, **AVR**, **PIC**, and **MSP430**, and each type has its own assembly language and instruction set architecture (ISA).

While microcontrollers generally use higher-level languages like C for development, Assembly is often used for low-level control, optimization, and when performance, size, and power consumption are critical.

2. Real-Time Constraints: How Assembly Helps Meet Timing Requirements in Embedded Systems

One of the defining characteristics of many embedded systems is the need to meet **real-time constraints**. In a real-time system, the correct operation depends not only on the logical correctness of the software but also on the timing of operations. For example, in automotive safety systems, the vehicle must react to sensor inputs within a very specific time window, or the system may fail.

2.1 What Are Real-Time Constraints?

Real-time constraints refer to the need for an embedded system to respond to inputs and events within a predetermined time frame. These constraints can be classified as:

- **Hard Real-Time**: In hard real-time systems, missing a deadline is considered a system failure. For example, a pacemaker must deliver a pulse to the heart at specific intervals to maintain a regular heartbeat.
- **Soft Real-Time**: In soft real-time systems, meeting deadlines is important but not absolutely critical. If a deadline is missed, the system can still function, but performance may degrade. For instance, video streaming systems may tolerate occasional delays without breaking the system.

2.2 The Role of Assembly in Meeting Timing Requirements

Assembly language is particularly useful in embedded systems where real-time constraints are critical. High-level languages like C are slower because they abstract away hardware details, which introduces overhead. Assembly language, on the other hand, provides direct control over the hardware, allowing developers to write highly optimized code that can meet the stringent timing requirements of real-time embedded systems.

In Assembly, you can fine-tune the timing of instructions and ensure that critical tasks are executed at the exact right time. Additionally, Assembly enables the use of hardware-specific features like timers, interrupts, and direct memory access (DMA), all of which can be crucial in meeting real-time requirements.

For example, an embedded system controlling a robotic arm may need to perform specific movements with precise timing. Assembly allows you to write code that interacts directly with the hardware to ensure that the arm moves within the required time frame.

3. Optimizing for Power Efficiency: Writing Assembly Code for Low-Power Systems

In many embedded systems, particularly in battery-powered devices like smartphones, wearables, and IoT devices, **power efficiency** is a primary concern. These systems need to operate for long periods without recharging or using excessive power.

3.1 The Importance of Power Efficiency in Embedded Systems

Power efficiency is a critical factor in embedded system design because these systems often need to operate continuously for extended periods while consuming as little energy as possible. A key component of power management is **dynamic power scaling**, where the system can adjust its power usage based on the current workload or activity level.

For example, an IoT sensor that measures environmental conditions may spend most of its time in a low-power sleep mode, only waking up periodically to take measurements. The challenge is to ensure that the sensor consumes minimal power while still being able to respond to events as needed.

3.2 How Assembly Helps Achieve Power Efficiency

Assembly language provides the programmer with direct control over hardware components, allowing for fine-grained power management. By writing Assembly code, developers can take advantage of low-level features of the microcontroller, such as putting the system into sleep mode, turning off unused peripherals, and adjusting clock speeds to save power.

In addition, Assembly allows developers to minimize the number of instructions executed, reducing the processing time and, in turn, the power consumption. High-level languages often introduce unnecessary overhead, whereas Assembly can provide the most efficient implementation for power-sensitive applications.

POWER EFFICIENCY TECHNIQUES IN ASSEMBLY

1. **Low-Power Modes**: Many microcontrollers feature different power states, such as sleep, idle, and deep sleep modes. Assembly allows you to control these power states directly, ensuring that the system is consuming as little power as possible when idle.
2. **Peripheral Control**: Embedded systems often have peripherals like sensors, displays, and communication modules. In Assembly, you can manage the power consumption of each peripheral, turning off unused peripherals to save energy.
3. **Clock Scaling**: Some microcontrollers allow dynamic adjustment of the clock speed. By slowing down the processor when full speed is not required, you can reduce power consumption.
4. **Interrupt-Driven Operation**: Instead of continuously polling for events, Assembly code can be written to handle events using interrupts, ensuring that the processor only consumes power when necessary.

4. Hands-On Example: Writing Assembly for an Embedded System to Control a Motor

Now that we have covered the theory behind Assembly in embedded systems, let's dive into a practical example: writing Assembly code to control a motor in an embedded system. We will use an **ARM microcontroller** as the platform for this example, although the concepts apply to many other microcontrollers as well.

4.1 Motor Control: The Basics

Motor control is a common application in embedded systems, from industrial robots to household appliances. Controlling a motor typically involves sending a signal to a motor driver that controls the speed and direction of the motor.

In this example, we will write Assembly code for a simple embedded system that controls the speed of a **DC motor** using **Pulse Width Modulation (PWM)**.

4.2 Understanding PWM

PWM is a technique used to control the speed of a motor by varying the duty cycle of a digital signal. The duty cycle refers to the proportion of time the signal is high versus low in each cycle. A higher duty cycle means the motor receives more power, which increases its speed.

For example, a PWM signal with a 50% duty cycle will turn the motor on for half the time and off for the other half, resulting in a moderate speed. A 75% duty cycle will make the motor run faster, as it receives power for 75% of the time.

4.3 Writing the Assembly Code

Let's assume we are using an ARM-based microcontroller to generate the PWM signal. The code will involve setting up a timer to generate the PWM signal and then controlling the motor speed based on the duty cycle.

```assembly
section .data
    duty_cycle db 50        ; PWM duty cycle (50% in
this case)

section .bss
    motor_pin resb 1        ; Motor control pin (set up
for PWM output)

section .text
    global _start

_start:
    ; Initialize PWM
    mov r0, 0x40010000    ; Address of the timer
register
    mov r1, 0x1000          ; Set timer period (example
value)
    str r1, [r0]            ; Write the timer period to
the register

    ; Set up the duty cycle
    mov r1, [duty_cycle]  ; Load the duty cycle into
register r1
    mul r1, r1, r0          ; Calculate the high time
for the PWM signal
    str r1, [motor_pin]    ; Set the motor pin to
output the PWM signal

    ; Loop to continue generating PWM signal
loop_start:
    ; Wait for the next PWM period
    b loop_start            ; Repeat the process to
maintain PWM signal
```

In this simplified example:

- We initialize a **timer register** to set the frequency of the PWM signal.
- The **duty cycle** is loaded into a register, and the motor's control pin is set to output the PWM signal based on that duty cycle.
- The code runs in a loop to continually generate the PWM signal, adjusting the motor speed accordingly.

4.4 Explanation of the Code

- **Timer Setup**: The timer register (`0x40010000`) is set to a specific value that controls the frequency of the PWM signal. This value will depend on the microcontroller's clock settings and the desired PWM frequency.
- **Duty Cycle Control**: The duty cycle is loaded from memory and used to calculate the high time of the PWM signal. This value is written to the motor control pin, which will toggle between high and low at the specified duty cycle.
- **Looping**: The program continuously loops to maintain the PWM signal. In real-world applications, you would typically use interrupts or a real-time operating system (RTOS) to handle timing more efficiently.

Conclusion

In this chapter, we explored the critical role that **Assembly language** plays in **embedded systems**. These systems, which are designed to perform specific tasks, require precise control over hardware, making Assembly an essential tool for developers working with microcontrollers and other embedded platforms. We covered the unique challenges of embedded systems, including real-time constraints and power efficiency, and discussed how Assembly can help meet these challenges with efficient, low-level code.

We also looked at practical examples, including controlling a motor with **PWM** in Assembly, which demonstrates how low-level code interacts directly with hardware to perform specific tasks efficiently. By using Assembly in embedded systems, developers gain full control over the hardware and can create systems that meet stringent timing, memory, and power requirements.

With the knowledge gained from this chapter, you can now start developing your own embedded systems using Assembly, taking full advantage of the performance and control it offers in these specialized applications.

CHAPTER 9: ASSEMBLY AND MACHINE CODE IN PERFORMANCE OPTIMIZATION

Introduction

When it comes to optimizing software performance, especially in critical applications where speed and efficiency are paramount, low-level programming languages like **Assembly** offer distinct advantages. Unlike high-level languages, which are abstracted from the hardware, **Assembly language** gives the programmer direct control over the CPU, memory, and other hardware components. This level of control enables the creation of highly optimized code that can push the boundaries of performance.

In this chapter, we will explore how **Assembly and machine code** can be used for performance optimization. We'll look at the reasons why low-level code can outperform high-level languages, delve into **profiling and benchmarking** techniques for identifying performance bottlenecks, and discuss **cache optimization** to ensure that programs make the best use of the CPU's cache. Finally, we will demonstrate these principles with a hands-on example, optimizing an image processing algorithm using Assembly to maximize speed and efficiency.

1. How Low-Level Code Enhances Performance: Why Assembly is Faster than High-Level Languages

The primary reason that **Assembly language** is often faster than high-level languages lies in its low-level nature. When writing code in high-level languages like Python, Java, or even C++, the compiler or interpreter must translate the high-level instructions into machine code. This process introduces overhead, both in terms of execution time and memory usage.

With **Assembly**, you're writing directly to the machine. The code you write is translated directly into machine instructions that the CPU can execute. There are no layers of abstraction, and you're in full control of every step in the process. Let's look at the specific reasons why Assembly tends to offer superior performance:

1.1 Direct Control Over Hardware

In high-level languages, many operations are abstracted from the programmer. For instance, memory management, variable storage, and other system-level operations are handled automatically by the language runtime or operating system. In contrast, Assembly language allows direct manipulation of hardware, meaning that the programmer can manage memory, registers, and I/O operations with complete precision.

For example, in Assembly, you can directly choose which registers to use and how to store values in memory. This allows you to minimize overhead and maximize efficiency.

1.2 No Unnecessary Abstractions

High-level languages often introduce abstractions, such as automatic garbage collection, dynamic memory management, and type checking, all of which can slow down execution. Assembly language operates without these abstractions, meaning that every instruction executed is purposeful, directly corresponding to a specific operation on the CPU. This results in faster execution time because no resources are wasted on managing abstractions that might not be needed for the task at hand.

1.3 Reduced Execution Overhead

High-level languages, especially those that rely on virtual machines (e.g., Java with the JVM, Python with the interpreter), incur execution overhead due to the need for runtime environments. In contrast, Assembly code is executed directly by the CPU, without any intermediary layers. This leads to significantly reduced execution time, particularly in performance-sensitive applications.

In addition, many high-level languages have a larger memory footprint because of built-in libraries and frameworks, whereas Assembly programs are minimal in size, which contributes to faster execution and reduced memory consumption.

1.4 Optimizing for Specific Hardware Architectures

Assembly allows you to write code that is tailored to the specific hardware architecture you are working with. For instance, when writing Assembly for an **x86** processor, you can take full advantage of the processor's instruction set, registers, and special features like **SIMD** (Single Instruction, Multiple Data). By optimizing your

Assembly code for the exact features of the hardware, you can achieve maximum performance.

In contrast, high-level languages are often designed to be cross-platform and abstract away hardware-specific optimizations. This makes high-level code more portable but sacrifices the ability to take full advantage of the underlying hardware.

2. Profiling and Benchmarking: Analyzing Performance Bottlenecks

Before you can optimize code, it is crucial to **measure** its performance. **Profiling** and **benchmarking** are key techniques for identifying the parts of a program that are slow and need improvement. These tools allow developers to analyze the runtime behavior of their programs and focus optimization efforts on the areas that will yield the greatest improvements.

2.1 Profiling: Understanding Code Behavior

Profiling is the process of collecting data about a program's execution, such as how long certain functions take to execute, how much memory is used, and how the CPU is utilized. Profiling tools can help you identify performance bottlenecks by showing which functions consume the most resources.

In Assembly, profiling can be done manually by inserting timing code at critical points in the program. For example, using a **timer register** or **cycle counter** in a microcontroller, you can measure how long specific blocks of code take to execute. Additionally, you can use

performance counters provided by modern processors to measure CPU usage, cache hits, and other low-level performance metrics.

Here's an example of how you might time a block of code in Assembly:

```assembly
; Start timing
rdtsc                   ; Read the time-stamp counter
into EDX:EAX

; Execute the code block you want to profile
; (code to be timed)

; End timing
rdtsc                   ; Read the time-stamp counter
again
sub edx, [start_time] ; Subtract the start time to
calculate elapsed time
```

This method uses the **Time-Stamp Counter (TSC)**, a special register that counts the number of CPU cycles since the system was powered on, allowing you to measure the time between two points in the code.

2.2 Benchmarking: Measuring Performance

Benchmarking involves running your program in a controlled environment and measuring its performance across different runs or different versions of the code. Benchmarking can help you understand how different optimizations affect the overall performance.

In embedded systems, benchmarking might involve measuring how quickly the system can respond to an event or process a task. For example, an embedded image processing algorithm could be benchmarked by measuring how long it takes to process an image of a certain size.

You can use tools like **perf** in Linux or **Intel VTune** to benchmark high-level and low-level code. These tools offer insight into CPU utilization, cache performance, and instruction-level bottlenecks.

2.3 Identifying Bottlenecks

A bottleneck is a part of the program that limits the overall performance. It can be a specific function that takes too long to execute, inefficient memory usage, or a part of the code that causes frequent cache misses. Identifying these bottlenecks is a crucial part of performance optimization.

Common sources of bottlenecks include:

- **Excessive branching**: Loops and conditional statements that force the CPU to constantly change its execution path can slow down execution, especially if they prevent the CPU from making use of pipelining.
- **Memory access**: Programs that frequently read and write to memory or that have poor memory locality can experience slowdowns due to cache misses.
- **Integer divisions and multiplications**: These operations can be slower than simple additions and subtractions, especially in older or simpler CPUs.

Once you've identified the bottlenecks, you can focus on optimizing those areas by reducing unnecessary operations, improving memory access patterns, or utilizing more efficient algorithms.

3. Cache Optimization: Writing Assembly Code to Optimize Cache Usage

Modern CPUs rely heavily on **cache memory** to improve performance. Cache memory is a small but fast type of memory located directly on the CPU. It stores frequently used data, allowing the CPU to access it more quickly than if it had to fetch it from main memory. However, cache memory is limited, so optimizing cache usage is crucial for maximizing performance, especially in assembly programming.

3.1 Understanding CPU Cache Hierarchy

Modern processors use a multi-level cache hierarchy, typically consisting of:

- **L1 Cache**: The fastest and smallest cache, located closest to the CPU core.
- **L2 Cache**: Larger than L1 cache, but slower.
- **L3 Cache**: Shared across multiple cores and significantly larger but slower than L1 and L2 caches.

In assembly programming, understanding how the CPU uses its cache can help you write more efficient code by ensuring that data is stored in a way that maximizes cache hits and minimizes cache misses.

3.2 Cache Optimization Techniques

Here are several techniques for optimizing cache usage in Assembly:

1. **Data Locality**:

- Spatial Locality: Accessing data that is located close to recently accessed data. To optimize for spatial locality, ensure that your data is arranged in contiguous memory blocks.
- Temporal Locality: Accessing the same data multiple times within a short period. Reuse data stored in registers instead of constantly accessing memory.

Example: When processing an array, instead of iterating over scattered memory locations, arrange the data so that related items are grouped together in memory. This increases the likelihood that when one item is accessed, the next item will also be in cache.

2. **Loop Optimization**:
   - **Loop unrolling**: Instead of executing a loop iteratively, you can unroll the loop, performing multiple operations within a single iteration. This reduces the overhead of jumping back to the loop and improves cache performance by reducing the number of instructions executed.

Example of loop unrolling:

```assembly
; Original loop
MOV ECX, 100          ; Loop counter
loop_start:
ADD AX, [arr + ECX]
DEC ECX
JNZ loop_start

; Unrolled loop
MOV ECX, 50           ; Loop counter
loop_unrolled:
ADD AX, [arr + ECX * 2]
```

```
ADD AX, [arr + ECX * 2 + 1]
DEC ECX
JNZ loop_unrolled
```

3. **Blocking**: When working with multi-dimensional arrays or matrices, accessing elements row by row is often more cache-friendly than accessing them column by column. This is because memory is typically organized in rows, and accessing data in this way maximizes cache hits.
4. **Prefetching**: Some processors allow manual prefetching of data into cache using special instructions. This can be particularly useful when you know that you'll need to access specific data soon and want to ensure that it's loaded into the cache ahead of time.

3.3 Minimizing Cache Misses

Cache misses occur when the CPU requests data that is not in the cache, forcing it to fetch data from slower main memory. To minimize cache misses:

- **Access data in chunks**: Accessing large blocks of memory at once increases the likelihood of cache hits.
- **Optimize memory layout**: When working with arrays or matrices, store them in row-major or column-major order depending on the access pattern.

4. Hands-on Example: Optimizing an Image Processing Algorithm Using Assembly

Now, let's apply the concepts we've learned in this chapter by optimizing an image processing algorithm using Assembly. The task will be to **invert an image**, which involves flipping each pixel's color value (e.g., from black to white, from red to green, etc.).

4.1 Basic Image Processing Algorithm

The basic algorithm for inverting an image involves iterating through each pixel, extracting its color values, and inverting them. Here's how you might write this in C:

c

```
for (int i = 0; i < image_width; i++) {
    for (int j = 0; j < image_height; j++) {
        image[i][j] = ~image[i][j];   // Invert the
color (bitwise NOT)
    }
}
```

In Assembly, this process can be optimized for speed and memory access. We'll focus on minimizing the number of memory accesses and maximizing cache hits by processing large chunks of data at once.

4.2 Optimizing with Assembly

Here's an Assembly version of the image inversion algorithm optimized for performance:

assembly

```
section .data
    image db 100, 200, 150, 255, 0   ; Example image
data (1D array for simplicity)
    image_size equ 5                  ; Size of the
image (5 pixels)

section .text
```

```
    global _start

_start:
    mov ecx, image_size   ; Set loop counter (number
of pixels)
    mov esi, image        ; Address of the image array

invert_loop:
    ; Load the current pixel value
    mov al, [esi]
    not al                ; Invert the pixel color
(bitwise NOT)
    mov [esi], al         ; Store the inverted value
back to memory

    inc esi               ; Move to the next pixel
    loop invert_loop      ; Repeat for all pixels

    ; Exit the program
    mov eax, 1            ; sys_exit
    xor ebx, ebx          ; exit code 0
    int 0x80             ; call the kernel
```

4.3 Explanation of Optimization

- **Memory Access:** Instead of accessing the image data one pixel at a time with high overhead, we use a simple loop that reads and writes the pixel data directly in a linear fashion. This helps maximize memory locality and ensures that the CPU can efficiently access memory in consecutive addresses.
- **Register Use:** We use the AL register to hold the pixel data while inverting it. This minimizes memory access by performing the operation in registers.
- **Loop Efficiency:** The loop is simple, with minimal branching. Each iteration only involves reading from memory, performing a bitwise operation, and writing the result back.

This simple yet efficient approach demonstrates how Assembly can be used to optimize even basic algorithms. By focusing on reducing memory accesses, using registers effectively, and keeping the loop structure simple, we have created a much faster implementation than the original high-level C code.

Conclusion

In this chapter, we explored the key techniques used to optimize performance in low-level programming with Assembly. We discussed how Assembly allows for direct control over the hardware, leading to faster execution compared to high-level languages. We also delved into **profiling and benchmarking** techniques to identify performance bottlenecks and explored **cache optimization** to ensure efficient memory access.

Finally, through the hands-on example of optimizing an image processing algorithm, we demonstrated how low-level optimizations—such as minimizing memory access, using registers efficiently, and simplifying loops—can lead to significant performance improvements. Whether working on embedded systems, high-performance computing, or systems programming, these optimization techniques are essential for writing fast and efficient Assembly code.

As you continue to develop your low-level programming skills, remember that **Assembly** provides the finest level of control, enabling you to squeeze every ounce of performance from the underlying hardware.

CHAPTER 10:
INTERFACING ASSEMBLY
WITH C/C++

Introduction

In modern software development, high-level languages like **C** and **C++** provide an efficient and flexible environment for creating applications. However, there are scenarios where **Assembly language** still holds a significant advantage due to its low-level access to hardware and ability to optimize critical sections of code. **Interfacing Assembly with C/C++** allows developers to take full advantage of both worlds: the efficiency and fine-grained control of Assembly, combined with the readability and portability of high-level languages like C and C++.

In this chapter, we will explore why and when you should combine **Assembly** with **C/C++**, how to write **inline Assembly** to insert small snippets of Assembly code within C or C++ programs, and how to properly **link** Assembly and C/C++ together in a single program. Finally, we'll work through a **hands-on example**, demonstrating how inline Assembly can be used to optimize a function written in C.

1. Why Combine Assembly with High-Level Languages?

Assembly language offers precise control over the processor and memory, enabling developers to write highly optimized code that meets strict performance, timing, or size requirements. However, it comes at the cost of reduced readability, portability, and maintainability. High-level languages like C and C++ provide abstraction, which simplifies development and ensures portability across different systems. So why combine them? The key is that **Assembly** can complement **C/C++** in areas where raw performance is necessary without sacrificing the higher-level features that C and C++ provide.

1.1 When to Use Assembly in C/C++

While C and C++ are incredibly powerful, they cannot always offer the fine control and efficiency that Assembly provides. Here are some specific situations when incorporating Assembly into a C or C++ program is beneficial:

- **Performance Optimization**: In some cases, performance-critical code—such as mathematical computations, encryption algorithms, or rendering routines—can be optimized using Assembly. By using Assembly, developers can take advantage of specific processor features such as SIMD (Single Instruction, Multiple Data) or low-level CPU instructions.
- **Hardware Access**: Assembly provides the ability to directly control hardware components such as I/O devices, memory-mapped registers, or specialized peripherals. In embedded systems or low-level system programming, Assembly allows developers to interact with hardware components directly from C or C++.
- **Real-Time Constraints**: In real-time systems where timing is critical, Assembly allows precise control over execution speed, ensuring that tasks meet strict deadlines. For example, in embedded systems like automotive controllers, Assembly can ensure that time-sensitive operations are executed in a specific order or within a specific time frame.
- **Legacy Code**: In some legacy systems or specialized hardware environments, parts of the codebase may still

need to be written in Assembly due to hardware-specific constraints or performance reasons. C/C++ can be used for higher-level application logic, while Assembly can be used for the low-level components.

1.2 Benefits of Using Assembly in C/C++

- **Performance**: The biggest benefit of using Assembly is performance. Critical loops, mathematical functions, and other performance-intensive tasks can often be written in Assembly to make them run faster than the equivalent C/C++ code.
- **Efficiency**: Assembly provides the ability to fine-tune code and manage resources, such as memory, with minimal overhead. This is especially important in environments with limited resources, such as embedded systems.
- **System-level Programming**: In systems programming, where access to hardware or low-level resources is required, Assembly provides the level of control needed. For instance, when writing device drivers, Assembly can be used to interact with hardware directly, while C/C++ is used to handle higher-level logic.

2. Inline Assembly: Writing Small Snippets of Assembly Inside C or C++ Code

One of the simplest ways to incorporate Assembly into a C or C++ program is through **inline Assembly**. Inline Assembly allows developers to write short snippets of Assembly code within the body of their C or C++ code. This is particularly useful when performance optimization is needed in a small portion of the program, without needing to write an entire Assembly file.

2.1 What is Inline Assembly?

Inline Assembly is a feature supported by most modern compilers that allows assembly code to be embedded directly in C or C++ source files. This allows you to write efficient, low-level code for small performance-critical sections without leaving the high-level language.

The syntax for inline Assembly varies between compilers, but the general format is similar. Here's an example of inline Assembly in GCC (GNU Compiler Collection) for x86 architecture:

c

```
int add_numbers(int a, int b) {
    int result;
    __asm__ (
        "addl %[input1], %[input2]\n\t"
        "movl %[input2], %[output]"
        : [output] "=r" (result)            // Output
operand
        : [input1] "r" (a), [input2] "r" (b)   //
Input operands
    );
    return result;
}
```

In this example, the `add_numbers` function uses inline Assembly to add two integers and store the result in the `result` variable. The `__asm__` block contains the Assembly code, while the colons separate the output operands, input operands, and clobbered registers (if any).

2.2 Benefits of Inline Assembly

- **Ease of Use**: Inline Assembly allows developers to insert low-level code directly into their existing C/C++ programs, making it easy to fine-tune specific sections of the code without needing to manage separate Assembly files.

- **Control**: With inline Assembly, you maintain full control over the registers and operations in that section of the program, which can lead to significant performance improvements.
- **Portability**: For portable, high-level codebases that require assembly optimizations, inline assembly provides a way to optimize performance without having to rewrite the entire program in Assembly. However, it's important to note that inline assembly code is often platform-specific and can reduce portability.

2.3 Considerations for Using Inline Assembly

While inline assembly provides performance advantages, there are some considerations to keep in mind:

- **Readability**: Inline Assembly can make your code harder to read and maintain. It's best used sparingly and only for critical sections that require optimization.
- **Debugging**: Debugging Assembly code can be more difficult than high-level languages because of the lack of abstractions and the intricacies of the assembly language syntax.
- **Compiler Restrictions**: Different compilers have different syntax and support for inline assembly. GCC and Clang are widely used, but some compilers may have more restrictive or different ways to handle inline assembly.

3. Linking Assembly and C: How to Mix Both Languages in One Program

Sometimes, inline Assembly is not sufficient, and you need to use full assembly files alongside C or C++ code. This can happen when large portions of the program require optimization, or when you need to implement low-level hardware interactions that are impractical in inline assembly.

To combine Assembly and C/C++ in the same program, you need to use an external assembly file that is **linked** with the C/C++ code. Here's a step-by-step overview of how you would do this:

3.1 Writing the Assembly Code

First, write the Assembly code in a separate file. Let's assume you're writing an Assembly function to perform bitwise operations:

```
assembly

; bitwise_operations.asm
section .text
    global bitwise_and
    global bitwise_or

bitwise_and:
    ; Perform bitwise AND between two integers
    mov eax, [esp+4]    ; Load the first parameter
into eax
    mov ebx, [esp+8]    ; Load the second parameter
into ebx
    and eax, ebx        ; Perform bitwise AND
    ret

bitwise_or:
    ; Perform bitwise OR between two integers
    mov eax, [esp+4]    ; Load the first parameter
into eax
    mov ebx, [esp+8]    ; Load the second parameter
into ebx
    or eax, ebx         ; Perform bitwise OR
    ret
```

This Assembly code defines two functions: `bitwise_and` and `bitwise_or`. Both functions take two parameters from the stack, perform the operation, and return the result in the `eax` register.

3.2 Linking Assembly with C

Next, you need to link this Assembly code with your C or C++ program. Here's an example of the C code that will call the assembly functions:

c

```c
#include <stdio.h>

extern int bitwise_and(int a, int b);   // Declare the
Assembly function
extern int bitwise_or(int a, int b);

int main() {
    int a = 5, b = 3;
    printf("Bitwise AND: %d\n", bitwise_and(a, b));
// Call the Assembly function
    printf("Bitwise OR: %d\n", bitwise_or(a, b));
// Call the Assembly function
    return 0;
}
```

The `extern` keyword tells the compiler that the `bitwise_and` and `bitwise_or` functions are defined externally (in Assembly in this case). When the program is compiled and linked, the Assembly functions will be included and executed when called from C.

3.3 Compiling and Linking the Program

To compile and link the C code and Assembly code together, you need to perform the following steps:

1. **Assemble the Assembly Code**: Use an assembler to convert the assembly file into an object file.

   bash

   ```
   nasm -f elf64 -o bitwise_operations.o
   bitwise_operations.asm
   ```

2. **Compile the C Code**: Use the C compiler to compile the C program into an object file.

   bash

   ```
   gcc -c -o main.o main.c
   ```

3. **Link the Object Files**: Finally, link the object files together to create the executable.

   bash

   ```
   gcc -o program main.o bitwise_operations.o
   ```

Now, when you run the program, it will use the Assembly functions to perform the bitwise operations.

---

4. Hands-on Example: Using Inline Assembly to Optimize a Function in C

To demonstrate how inline Assembly can be used to optimize a function, let's take a simple example: a function to compute the

Greatest Common Divisor (GCD) of two numbers using the
Euclidean algorithm.

4.1 The Euclidean Algorithm

The Euclidean algorithm for finding the greatest common divisor of
two numbers is simple:

1. Divide the larger number by the smaller number.
2. If the remainder is 0, the divisor is the GCD.
3. If the remainder is not 0, replace the larger number with the
   smaller number and the smaller number with the remainder,
   then repeat the process.

Here's a simple C implementation of this algorithm:

c

```
int gcd(int a, int b) {
    while (b != 0) {
        int temp = b;
        b = a % b;
        a = temp;
    }
    return a;
}
```

This function works fine, but it can be optimized with Assembly,
particularly for the modulus operation.

4.2 Optimizing with Inline Assembly

We can optimize the modulus operation by directly using Assembly
to perform the division and remainder calculation. Here's an
optimized version of the GCD function using inline Assembly:

c

```
int gcd(int a, int b) {
    while (b != 0) {
        __asm__ (
            "movl %1, %%eax;"   // Move a into eax
            "xchg %%eax, %0;"   // Exchange a and b
            "divl %%ebx;"       // Divide eax by b,
result in eax, remainder in edx
            "movl %%edx, %1;"   // Move remainder into
b
            : "=r" (a), "=r" (b)   // Output operands
            : "r" (a), "r" (b)     // Input operands
            : "%eax", "%ebx", "%edx"   // Clobbered
registers
        );
    }
    return a;
}
```

4.3 Explanation of the Code

- **Inline Assembly Block**: The code block inside __asm__
  contains the Assembly instructions that directly manipulate
  the registers (eax, ebx, edx) and perform the modulus
  calculation.
- **xchg Instruction**: The xchg instruction exchanges the values
  in two registers. This is used to swap the values of a and b to
  match the order required by the Euclidean algorithm.
- **div Instruction**: The div instruction divides eax by the value
  in ebx and stores the quotient in eax and the remainder in
  edx. We store the remainder (in edx) back into b.

4.4 Conclusion

In this example, we used inline Assembly to optimize the modulus
operation, which is the most performance-critical part of the GCD
calculation. By using **Assembly** directly, we can execute the

modulus operation more efficiently, which can be particularly beneficial in embedded systems or other performance-sensitive environments.

Conclusion

In this chapter, we explored the integration of **Assembly language** with **C/C++**, focusing on why combining these languages can lead to optimal performance and better hardware control. We discussed **inline assembly**, where small snippets of Assembly code are inserted directly into C/C++ code to optimize specific sections. We also covered how to **link Assembly and C** to build more complex systems where both languages work together. The hands-on examples provided insight into how **inline assembly** can be used to improve function performance, such as optimizing the **GCD algorithm**.

By incorporating **Assembly** into C/C++ code, developers gain the flexibility to write highly efficient, optimized programs that leverage the strengths of both high-level and low-level programming. Understanding when and how to use **Assembly** in conjunction with **C/C++** enables you to achieve performance gains in areas that require precise control over hardware, memory, and computation.

CHAPTER 11: ASSEMBLY IN MODERN ARCHITECTURES (X86 AND ARM)

Introduction

In the world of low-level programming, understanding how assembly language interacts with the underlying hardware architecture is essential for writing highly optimized code. **x86** and **ARM** are two of the most widely used **Instruction Set Architectures (ISAs)** in modern computing, each with its distinct features, design philosophies, and optimizations. While x86 has long been the dominant architecture for desktops, laptops, and servers, **ARM** has risen to prominence in the world of mobile devices, embedded systems, and increasingly in high-performance computing.

This chapter will explore **x86 assembly**, with a focus on its key concepts and how it differs from other ISAs, particularly **ARM architecture**, which has become a major force in mobile and embedded systems. We will also discuss how to write efficient assembly code for both **x86** and **ARM** processors, and examine the differences in performance characteristics between the two. Finally, we will work through a hands-on example, comparing assembly code for both x86 and ARM architectures, highlighting how these two platforms can be optimized for performance.

1. x86 Assembly: Key Concepts and Differences from Other ISAs

x86 refers to a family of ISAs developed by **Intel** and later adopted by other manufacturers like **AMD**. It has been the dominant architecture in personal computing, powering everything from desktop PCs to servers. Despite its age, x86 remains a powerful and highly capable architecture, continuously evolving with new features like **64-bit processing** (x86-64) and **vector processing** capabilities like **SSE** (Streaming SIMD Extensions).

1.1 The Evolution of x86 Architecture

The x86 architecture originated in the late 1970s with the **Intel 8086**, a 16-bit processor. Over time, it has evolved to support 32-bit and 64-bit processing, with each iteration maintaining backward compatibility with earlier versions of the architecture. Today's **x86-64** processors, which are 64-bit, still execute 32-bit and 16-bit code, a feature that allows x86 processors to run older software seamlessly.

The **x86 architecture** has expanded to support more complex features like:

- **SIMD (Single Instruction, Multiple Data)**: x86 supports SIMD instructions, which allow a single instruction to process multiple pieces of data simultaneously. This is particularly useful in applications like video encoding, gaming, and scientific computations.
- **Virtualization**: Modern x86 processors have hardware support for virtualization, allowing for the efficient execution of virtual machines.

- **Out-of-Order Execution**: x86 processors can execute instructions out of order to maximize throughput, making them capable of achieving high performance for certain workloads.

1.2 Key Concepts of x86 Assembly

When programming in x86 assembly, you interact directly with the processor's registers, flags, and memory. Some of the key concepts include:

- **Registers**: Registers are small, fast storage locations within the CPU. In x86 assembly, there are several types of registers:
  - **General-purpose registers** like AX, BX, CX, and DX.
  - **Special-purpose registers** such as the **Program Counter (PC)**, **Stack Pointer (SP)**, and **Instruction Pointer (IP)**.
  - **Flags Register**: Holds status flags such as Zero Flag (ZF), Carry Flag (CF), and Sign Flag (SF) to indicate the results of arithmetic or logical operations.
- **Memory Addressing Modes**: x86 supports a variety of addressing modes to access data in memory, such as:
  - **Immediate Addressing**: Using a constant value directly in an instruction.
  - **Direct Addressing**: Accessing a memory location directly.
  - **Indirect Addressing**: Using a register to store the address of the data.
  - **Indexed Addressing**: Using a base address plus an offset (commonly used for arrays).
- **Control Flow**: The **JMP** (jump) instruction is used to control the flow of execution, enabling loops, conditionals, and function calls. Other control flow instructions like **CALL** and **RET** are used for subroutine calls.

1.3 Differences Between x86 and Other ISAs

The most notable difference between **x86** and other ISAs, such as **ARM**, is its **Complex Instruction Set Computing (CISC)** nature. CISC architectures like x86 use complex instructions that can perform multiple operations in a single instruction. In contrast, **RISC** (Reduced Instruction Set Computing) architectures like ARM use a smaller, more streamlined set of simpler instructions.

- **Instruction Set Complexity**: x86 instructions can vary in length, and many instructions perform multiple operations (e.g., **MOV** can move data, perform arithmetic, and interact with memory). In ARM, most instructions are uniform in length, and simpler operations are performed with fewer instructions.
- **Register Usage**: x86 has a relatively small set of general-purpose registers compared to ARM. The limited number of registers in x86 necessitates frequent memory accesses in some cases, while ARM's larger register set allows for better utilization of registers and fewer memory accesses.
- **Energy Efficiency**: ARM architecture is designed with **energy efficiency** in mind, making it ideal for mobile and embedded devices. While x86 processors can be very powerful, they tend to consume more power, especially in high-performance desktop or server environments.

2. ARM Architecture: The Rise of ARM in Mobile and Embedded Systems

ARM (Advanced RISC Machines) is a family of ISAs designed with the principles of **RISC** in mind. Unlike x86's CISC approach, ARM focuses on a smaller and more efficient set of instructions, making it highly suitable for devices where power consumption and heat dissipation are major concerns. ARM processors are found in the majority of **mobile devices** (smartphones, tablets) and are gaining popularity in embedded systems and even high-performance computing.

2.1 The Key to ARM's Success: Simplicity and Efficiency

The ARM architecture emphasizes efficiency, simplicity, and low power consumption. Some of the key features of ARM include:

- **RISC Design**: ARM's Reduced Instruction Set Computing philosophy means it uses simpler instructions, leading to fewer clock cycles per instruction and reduced power consumption. ARM's instructions are typically of fixed length, which makes it easier to decode and execute quickly.
- **Register Set**: ARM processors have a larger number of general-purpose registers compared to x86 processors. This allows ARM to execute more operations using registers and minimizes the need for expensive memory accesses.
- **Low Power Consumption**: ARM processors are optimized for low power consumption, which makes them ideal for battery-powered devices. This is particularly important in mobile and embedded systems where battery life is critical.

2.2 ARM's Dominance in Mobile and Embedded Systems

ARM has become the dominant architecture for mobile devices, largely due to its energy efficiency. Companies like **Apple**, **Qualcomm**, and **Samsung** use ARM-based processors in their smartphones, tablets, and wearables. ARM is also widely used in **embedded systems**, powering everything from industrial control systems to IoT devices and medical equipment.

- **Customizable Core Designs**: ARM allows companies to design custom cores based on the ARM architecture, enabling them to fine-tune the performance and power efficiency for their specific needs. This has led to the widespread adoption of ARM in custom-designed chips (like Apple's **A-series** processors).

- **Ecosystem and Software Support**: ARM has a rich ecosystem, with extensive software libraries and development tools. The availability of **open-source software** and a variety of **real-time operating systems** (RTOS) tailored for ARM makes it easy for developers to create and optimize applications for ARM-based platforms.

2.3 ARM's Growth in High-Performance Computing

Recently, ARM has begun to make its way into **high-performance computing (HPC)**. With the rise of **ARM-based servers** and powerful processors like the **Apple M1**, ARM is now being considered as a viable alternative to x86 in data centers and servers. ARM's energy efficiency and scalability make it an attractive choice for cloud computing and edge computing applications.

3. Writing Efficient Code for Both: How to Optimize Assembly for Different CPUs

When writing **assembly code** for **x86** and **ARM**, it's essential to understand the differences in their instruction sets, register layouts, and execution models. Optimization for each architecture requires a tailored approach, but the goal is the same: write code that is efficient, fast, and utilizes the hardware to its fullest potential.

3.1 Register Usage and Memory Access

One of the main differences between x86 and ARM is the number of registers available. **ARM** has more general-purpose registers (e.g., **R0-R12**), while **x86** has fewer general-purpose registers (e.g., **AX,**

BX, CX). This makes **ARM** more efficient for certain tasks because more operations can be carried out in registers without needing to access memory.

For **x86**, you need to be mindful of the limited number of registers. Often, developers use the **stack** to hold intermediate values, which can slow down performance. **ARM**, with its larger register set, allows for better register usage and can help reduce memory access.

3.2 Instruction Set Efficiency

The instructions in **ARM** are generally simpler than those in **x86**. For example, ARM has a simple instruction set, and each instruction typically does one thing. In contrast, x86 instructions can be more complex and perform multiple operations in a single instruction.

- **ARM Optimization**: When optimizing for ARM, focus on using **load/store** instructions efficiently, as well as utilizing the extensive **SIMD** (Single Instruction, Multiple Data) capabilities available in modern ARM processors. ARM also provides specific instructions to handle floating-point operations, making it easier to optimize math-heavy tasks.
- **x86 Optimization**: For x86, take advantage of **SIMD extensions** like **SSE** and **AVX** to accelerate vector operations. These extensions allow multiple data elements to be processed in parallel, improving performance for tasks like multimedia processing and scientific computing.

3.3 Cache and Memory Optimization

Both x86 and ARM architectures rely on memory hierarchies that include **L1, L2, and L3 caches**, as well as main memory. Optimizing memory access patterns is key to writing efficient assembly code for both architectures.

- **ARM**: ARM's cache architecture is designed to be efficient in both high-performance and low-power applications. Use **cache-friendly** data structures and access patterns to minimize cache misses. Since ARM processors often feature smaller caches compared to high-performance x86 processors, optimizing memory locality is critical.
- **x86**: On the x86 platform, modern processors have **large caches** and high bandwidth. Optimizing for **data locality** and ensuring that loops and functions access memory sequentially will improve cache utilization. In high-performance x86 systems, cache **pipelining** and **prefetching** can help ensure that memory accesses are efficient.

---

4. Hands-On Example: Writing Assembly Code for Both x86 and ARM to Compare Performance

To put theory into practice, let's compare **assembly code for an algorithm**—specifically a **simple matrix multiplication**—for both **x86** and **ARM** to analyze performance differences.

4.1 Matrix Multiplication Algorithm

Matrix multiplication is a standard algorithm in scientific computing, often used in simulations, image processing, and machine learning. The basic idea is to multiply two matrices and store the result in a third matrix.

4.2 x86 Assembly Code for Matrix Multiplication

```
assembly
```

```
section .data
    matrix1 db 1, 2, 3, 4
    matrix2 db 5, 6, 7, 8
    result db 0, 0, 0, 0

section .text
    global _start

_start:
    ; Load first matrix value into eax
    mov al, [matrix1]
    mov bl, [matrix2]
    mul bl

    ; Store result into result matrix
    mov [result], al
    ; Repeat for other elements (omitted for brevity)
    ; ...
    mov eax, 1
    xor ebx, ebx
    int 0x80
```

4.3 ARM Assembly Code for Matrix Multiplication

```
assembly

section .data
    matrix1: .word 1, 2, 3, 4
    matrix2: .word 5, 6, 7, 8
    result:  .word 0, 0, 0, 0

section .text
    global _start

_start:
    ldr r0, [matrix1]        ; Load matrix1 element
into r0
    ldr r1, [matrix2]        ; Load matrix2 element
into r1
    mul r2, r0, r1           ; Multiply r0 and r1 and
store result in r2
    str r2, [result]         ; Store result in memory
```

```
; Repeat for other elements (omitted for brevity)
mov r7, #1              ; Exit system call
swi 0                   ; System call to exit
```

4.4 Performance Comparison

To compare the performance of these two implementations, we can use profiling tools like **perf** in Linux or **GDB** to measure execution time. On ARM devices, you would use tools like **QEMU** or **gprof** to perform similar profiling.

In both cases, optimizing the code for efficient memory access and using SIMD instructions where available would be key to improving performance.

Conclusion

In this chapter, we explored the differences between **x86** and **ARM** architectures, their respective assembly language programming paradigms, and how to write efficient code for both. We covered key concepts such as registers, memory access patterns, and the differences between **RISC** (ARM) and **CISC** (x86) design philosophies.

We also provided practical examples, including optimizing assembly code for both **x86** and **ARM**, to help highlight the performance advantages and challenges of each architecture. Whether you're working with mobile devices, embedded systems, or high-performance computing, understanding the nuances of each architecture is essential for writing fast, efficient, and portable assembly code.

By leveraging **Assembly language** for both **x86** and **ARM**, developers can write highly optimized software that maximizes hardware performance, making it possible to meet the stringent requirements of modern computing applications.

CHAPTER 12: LOW-LEVEL SECURITY AND EXPLOITS

Introduction

In the world of low-level programming, security vulnerabilities are often closely tied to the way data is handled at the hardware level. These vulnerabilities, which arise in systems programming, especially in **Assembly** language, are at the root of many of the most critical security exploits seen in the software industry. **Buffer overflows, stack smashing**, and advanced techniques like **Return-Oriented Programming (ROP)** are all methods that attackers can use to manipulate memory and control program execution.

In this chapter, we will explore these low-level security exploits, starting with **buffer overflows** and how they can be triggered in Assembly code. We'll look at **stack smashing** and **ROP**, and how attackers use them to bypass system protections. Finally, we'll cover techniques for writing secure Assembly code, preventing these vulnerabilities, and mitigating the risks of common low-level security exploits. We will also work through a **hands-on example**, demonstrating how a basic buffer overflow exploit works and how to prevent it using defensive programming techniques.

1. Buffer Overflows: How Assembly Interacts with Security Vulnerabilities

A **buffer overflow** is one of the most common and dangerous security vulnerabilities in low-level programming, often caused by improper handling of user input or memory allocation. It occurs when data overflows from one memory buffer to another, potentially overwriting the program's control structures like return addresses, leading to **arbitrary code execution**.

1.1 What is a Buffer Overflow?

In simple terms, a buffer overflow happens when a program writes more data into a buffer (a reserved memory space) than it was allocated to hold. The excess data spills over into adjacent memory regions, which can overwrite critical program data, such as **function return addresses**, **variables**, or **control flow information**.

For example, imagine a function that reads input into a fixed-size buffer:

assembly

```
; Simple buffer that can hold up to 10 bytes
buffer db 10 dup(0)

; Read user input into the buffer
mov eax, 3          ; sys_read system call number
mov ebx, 0          ; file descriptor (stdin)
mov ecx, buffer     ; address of the buffer
mov edx, 10         ; size of the buffer
int 0x80            ; invoke the system call
```

If the user inputs more than 10 bytes, the excess data will overwrite memory locations that were not meant to be modified. This can lead to unexpected behavior, and in some cases, it can allow an attacker to **control the flow of the program**.

1.2 How Does a Buffer Overflow Work?

A buffer overflow works by **corrupting the program's control data**, typically the **stack**, which stores function call return addresses. When a buffer is overrun, an attacker can overwrite the return address of a function, causing the program to jump to an arbitrary location in memory, where malicious code could reside.

For example:

1. **Normal Execution**: The program calls a function, and the return address is saved onto the stack.
2. **Overflow**: If a buffer overflow occurs, the attacker can overwrite the return address with the address of the attacker's payload or malicious code.
3. **Execution of Malicious Code**: When the function returns, it jumps to the attacker-controlled address, executing the malicious code.

This process is often used to gain unauthorized access or control over a system.

1.3 Example of a Buffer Overflow Exploit

Consider the following vulnerable C code:

c

```
#include <stdio.h>
#include <string.h>

void vulnerable_function(char *input) {
    char buffer[50];
```

```
    strcpy(buffer, input);   // Buffer overflow
vulnerability
}

int main() {
    char input[100];
    printf("Enter input: ");
    gets(input);   // Unsafe input handling
    vulnerable_function(input);
    return 0;
}
```

In this example:

- The **strcpy** function does not check the size of the input, leading to a buffer overflow if the input is larger than the allocated buffer.
- The **gets** function, which also doesn't check the input size, exacerbates the problem.

An attacker can input more than 50 characters, causing a **buffer overflow**, potentially overwriting the **return address** of the vulnerable_function. This could lead to the execution of malicious code.

2. Stack Smashing and Return-Oriented Programming (ROP): Exploiting Low-Level Code

2.1 Stack Smashing

Stack smashing is a specific type of buffer overflow where the overflowed data overwrites the return address of a function on the call stack. This enables attackers to modify the program's execution flow by hijacking function returns and redirecting the program to malicious code.

2.2 Return-Oriented Programming (ROP)

Return-Oriented Programming (ROP) is an advanced exploitation technique that bypasses traditional security defenses like **NX (No eXecute)** and **ASLR (Address Space Layout Randomization)**. Instead of injecting malicious code into the memory, **ROP** involves chaining together small pieces of existing code, called **gadgets**, which end with a return instruction.

In a typical buffer overflow attack, the attacker might try to inject shellcode into the stack. However, modern systems often have protections such as NX, which prevents the execution of code in certain memory regions (such as the stack). **ROP** bypasses this by reusing small fragments of legitimate code already present in the program or shared libraries.

- **Gadgets** are sequences of instructions that end with a return instruction (e.g., `RET` in x86).
- **ROP chains** are constructed by linking multiple gadgets together to perform a malicious operation.

By exploiting ROP, attackers can bypass security mechanisms and execute arbitrary code without injecting new code into memory.

3. Defensive Programming in Assembly: Writing Secure Assembly Code

Writing secure **Assembly** code requires an awareness of common vulnerabilities and the application of **defensive programming techniques** to mitigate risks. While Assembly language offers fine-grained control over hardware, it also requires careful management of memory and control structures to prevent vulnerabilities like buffer overflows, stack smashing, and other exploits.

3.1 Safe Memory Handling

One of the primary causes of vulnerabilities in low-level programming is improper memory handling. To write secure Assembly code, ensure that buffers are large enough to hold the data they are intended to store. Also, always validate input data before using it.

Examples:

- **Bounds Checking**: Before ing data into a buffer, check that the input does not exceed the buffer size.
- **Stack Canaries**: Use canary values (random values placed on the stack) to detect stack smashing before it happens.

3.2 Avoiding Dangerous Functions

Certain high-risk functions, like `strcpy`, `gets`, and `scanf`, should be avoided or used with caution because they do not check the size of input. These functions are often the source of buffer overflow vulnerabilities.

In Assembly, use safer, low-level memory operations that explicitly check the bounds before writing to memory.

3.3 Using Stack Protections

Many modern systems employ **stack protection mechanisms** to prevent buffer overflows and stack smashing attacks. These include:

- **Stack Canaries**: A value placed before the return address on the stack. If the canary value is overwritten by a buffer overflow, the program will detect it and terminate before executing malicious code.

- **Non-Executable Stack**: Modern systems use **NX (No eXecute)** to mark the stack as non-executable, preventing shellcode from running.
- **Address Space Layout Randomization (ASLR)**: Randomizes memory addresses to make it harder for an attacker to predict where specific data structures or functions are located.

3.4 Code Signing and Integrity Checks

In embedded systems and low-level applications, code integrity can be ensured by **code signing** and **hashing** techniques. By verifying the integrity of the program before execution, you can ensure that the program has not been modified maliciously.

---

4. Hands-on Example: Writing a Basic Buffer Overflow Exploit and Mitigating It

Now, let's work through an example of both writing a **basic buffer overflow exploit** and implementing a **mitigation** in Assembly. This hands-on example will help illustrate the concepts we've discussed and show how to address security vulnerabilities in low-level code.

4.1 Writing the Exploit

We will start by writing a simple C program with a **buffer overflow vulnerability**:

c

```
#include <stdio.h>
#include <string.h>
```

```
void vulnerable_function(char *input) {
    char buffer[32];
    strcpy(buffer, input);   // Buffer overflow
vulnerability
}

int main() {
    char input[128];
    printf("Enter input: ");
    gets(input);   // Unsafe input handling
    vulnerable_function(input);
    return 0;
}
```

In this vulnerable code, we have a buffer of size 32 bytes, but the `strcpy` function does not check the size of the input. An attacker can provide more than 32 characters and overwrite the return address.

EXPLOIT CODE:

An attacker can exploit this vulnerability by sending an input longer than 32 characters, causing the return address of `vulnerable_function` to be overwritten, potentially with the address of malicious shellcode.

For demonstration purposes, assume the return address is located at an offset of 36 bytes (this will vary depending on the system). The attacker can input a string that overwrites the return address and redirects the program to execute malicious code.

```bash
python -c 'print "A"*36 + "\xef\xbe\xad\xde"' |
./vulnerable_program
```

Here, `"\xef\xbe\xad\xde"` is a placeholder for the address of the attacker's shellcode. This string will overflow the buffer and overwrite the return address.

4.2 Mitigating the Vulnerability

Now that we've written the exploit, we will demonstrate how to mitigate it using **defensive programming** techniques in Assembly. Specifically, we will:

1. **Check the buffer size** before ing data into it.
2. **Use stack canaries** to detect stack smashing.
3. **Use safer memory functions** that ensure bounds checking.

Here's a modified version of the vulnerable function with mitigations in Assembly:

```assembly
assembly

section .data
    canary db 0xDE, 0xAD, 0xBE, 0xEF  ; Stack canary
value

section .bss
    buffer resb 32  ; 32-byte buffer to hold input

section .text
    global _start

_start:
    ; Set up the stack frame
    push ebp
    mov eax, [esp + 4]   ; Get the input pointer
    mov ecx, [eax]       ; Get the length of input
    cmp ecx, 32          ; Check if input length
exceeds buffer size
    jg overflow_detected

    ; Proceed with safe input handling
```

```
    mov edx, [eax + 4]   ; Move input to buffer safely
    ; (Perform actual input ing and handling here)
    jmp done

overflow_detected:
    ; Handle the overflow case (e.g., terminate the
program or report error)
    mov eax, 1  ; Exit system call
    xor ebx, ebx
    int 0x80

done:
    ; Return from function (safe execution)
    pop ebp
    ret
```

This code adds a **stack canary** to detect any overflow and terminates the program if the input is too large, preventing the overflow from overwriting the return address.

Conclusion

In this chapter, we covered the fundamentals of low-level security exploits and how they relate to **Assembly language.** We explored **buffer overflows, stack smashing**, and **Return-Oriented Programming (ROP)** as common attack vectors. We also discussed various defensive programming techniques to write secure Assembly code, including bounds checking, stack canaries, and using safer memory functions.

Through the **hands-on example**, we demonstrated both the exploitation of a basic buffer overflow vulnerability and how to mitigate it using **defensive Assembly programming techniques**. As low-level programming often interacts directly with memory and system resources, being aware of these vulnerabilities and knowing how to mitigate them is crucial for writing secure and robust code in Assembly.

By mastering these concepts, you can not only understand how low-level security exploits work but also be prepared to defend against them by writing secure, efficient, and reliable Assembly code.

CHAPTER 13: THE FUTURE OF ASSEMBLY AND MACHINE LANGUAGE

Introduction

Assembly language has long been regarded as the backbone of low-level programming, providing developers with direct control over hardware and performance optimization. However, in the face of modern **high-level languages**, the role of Assembly has evolved significantly. Today, **high-level languages** such as Python, Java, and C++ dominate the software development landscape due to their ease of use, portability, and powerful abstractions. Despite this shift, Assembly language still retains a niche role, especially in systems programming, embedded devices, and situations requiring raw performance and control.

In this chapter, we will explore the evolving landscape of Assembly and machine language in the context of modern technological trends. We'll examine the decline of **pure Assembly**, its place in the era of **virtualization**, and the exciting possibilities of **quantum computing**. Finally, we will dive into a hands-on example of how Assembly might be used in **quantum simulation**, demonstrating how low-level programming is adapting to the emerging field of quantum computing.

1. The Decline of Pure Assembly: High-Level Languages' Dominance and Assembly's Niche Role

Assembly language has long been a vital tool for developers working close to the hardware, but in recent decades, high-level languages have taken over the bulk of software development. As software systems grow increasingly complex, high-level languages like **C**, **C++**, **Java**, and **Python** provide powerful abstractions that make programming more efficient and accessible.

1.1 The Rise of High-Level Languages

The evolution of **high-level languages** can be traced back to the 1950s with languages like **Fortran** and **Lisp**, which offered abstraction over machine code, making it easier for programmers to focus on logic rather than hardware specifics. Over time, languages such as **C**, **C++**, and more recently **Python** have become the go-to choice for building software, offering a balance of performance, portability, and ease of use.

The key advantages of high-level languages are:

- **Abstraction**: High-level languages abstract away the complexities of memory management, CPU instruction sets, and hardware specifics. This allows developers to write code that is easier to understand and maintain.
- **Portability**: Programs written in high-level languages are typically portable across multiple platforms. A C or Java program, for example, can run on different types of CPUs without modification, thanks to the compiler or virtual machine (VM) abstraction.
- **Speed of Development**: High-level languages provide powerful libraries, frameworks, and tools that speed up the

development process. These languages allow developers to focus on solving business problems rather than managing memory or optimizing low-level instructions.

1.2 The Role of Assembly in the Modern Era

Despite the dominance of high-level languages, **Assembly** has not disappeared entirely. It still holds a crucial role in areas that require precise control over hardware and performance optimization, such as **embedded systems, systems programming,** and **performance-critical applications**. Assembly allows developers to interact directly with the machine, providing them with an unparalleled level of control over memory and CPU usage.

Assembly's Niche Role Today:

- **Embedded Systems**: In embedded systems, where resources like memory, power, and processing power are limited, Assembly remains the language of choice. It is used to optimize code for devices with very limited resources, such as **IoT devices, microcontrollers,** and **real-time systems**.
- **Performance-Critical Systems**: Some applications, such as game engines, multimedia processing, and cryptography, require the high performance that Assembly provides. In these cases, developers may write specific routines in Assembly to take full advantage of the hardware's capabilities.
- **Operating Systems and Kernels**: Parts of operating systems, particularly those that interact with the hardware directly (like device drivers and kernel code), are still written in Assembly for maximum efficiency.

While Assembly is no longer the primary language for most software applications, its ability to directly interface with hardware ensures it remains relevant in certain domains.

2. Assembly in the Age of Virtualization: How Virtual Machines and Containers Impact Low-Level Programming

With the rise of **virtualization** and **containerization**, the landscape of low-level programming is changing. These technologies allow for the creation of isolated environments (virtual machines and containers) that run software independently of the host operating system, providing a level of abstraction between software and hardware. This abstraction layer has significant implications for how Assembly interacts with the underlying hardware.

2.1 Virtualization and Its Impact on Low-Level Programming

Virtualization allows multiple operating systems (OSes) to run on a single physical machine simultaneously. This is achieved by creating a **hypervisor**, a layer of software that controls the hardware resources and allocates them to virtual machines (VMs). The hypervisor abstracts the hardware from the guest operating systems, meaning that the virtualized environment does not have direct access to the hardware in the same way as traditional systems.

In a virtualized environment, **Assembly programming** becomes more complex due to the abstraction. For instance:

- **Direct Hardware Access**: In a virtual machine, the guest OS cannot access the hardware directly. Instead, it must make calls to the hypervisor, which then translates those requests into operations that the physical hardware can understand. This creates an additional layer between Assembly code and the hardware.
- **Resource Management**: Assembly code that was originally optimized to interact with physical hardware must now account for the virtualization layer. For example, memory access must be managed in a way that is compatible with the virtualized memory model, and I/O operations must be directed to the hypervisor rather than directly to the hardware.

Despite these challenges, **virtual machines** and **hypervisors** have also created new opportunities for low-level programming. Developers writing low-level code for VMs or hypervisors must understand the interaction between the guest OS and the host system and optimize their code accordingly.

2.2 Containers and Their Impact on Low-Level Programming

Containers, such as those provided by **Docker**, offer another layer of abstraction that has become extremely popular for deploying and managing applications. Unlike virtual machines, which virtualize the entire hardware stack, containers virtualize the operating system, allowing multiple isolated environments to run on the same host OS.

While containers are more lightweight than virtual machines, they still introduce some abstraction, particularly in terms of networking, storage, and resource allocation. For developers working with low-level code in containers, the challenge is to optimize performance within this containerized environment while managing resource usage and interaction with the host system.

For example, while Assembly code inside a container can still interact with the CPU and memory, it must respect the limits imposed by the container's resource allocation, such as CPU cores, memory, and I/O bandwidth. This adds an extra layer of complexity when trying to optimize assembly code for containers.

3. Quantum Computing: The Future of Low-Level Programming in Quantum Systems

Quantum computing represents a revolutionary shift in the way we think about computing. Unlike classical computers, which rely on bits as the basic unit of information (either 0 or 1), quantum computers use **quantum bits** or **qubits**, which can exist in multiple states simultaneously. This allows quantum computers to perform certain types of computations much faster than classical computers.

3.1 Quantum Computers and Low-Level Programming

Low-level programming in the realm of quantum computing is fundamentally different from traditional assembly and machine language programming. Quantum computers rely on quantum gates and circuits to manipulate qubits, and programming these systems requires a different approach.

However, understanding the role of low-level programming in quantum computing is crucial. While quantum algorithms like **Shor's algorithm** and **Grover's algorithm** are usually written in high-level quantum programming languages like **Qiskit** or **Quipper**, low-level quantum control often requires a deep understanding of quantum gates, qubit entanglement, and decoherence.

3.2 Quantum Machine Language

Just as classical assembly language directly interacts with the hardware through machine code, quantum machine language (QML) will interact with quantum processors. While quantum programming languages today are abstracted to high-level commands, they eventually compile down to a set of quantum instructions that manipulate qubits.

Low-level programming in quantum computing involves:

- **Quantum gates**: These are the basic operations that manipulate qubits. Gates like **Hadamard (H)**, **CNOT**, and **Pauli-X** are the quantum equivalents of classical logic gates.
- **Quantum circuits**: Quantum gates are applied in sequence to form quantum circuits, which perform computations.
- **Quantum hardware interaction**: To run quantum programs on real quantum machines, low-level programming often involves the management of qubits, error correction, and physical control of quantum devices.

3.3 Writing Assembly for Quantum Simulation on Classical Machines

While true quantum machines are still in the early stages of development, **quantum simulators** on classical machines are available to test and develop quantum algorithms. These simulators provide a way to write quantum programs that behave similarly to how they would on a quantum computer.

Here's an example of how low-level programming concepts could be applied to simulate a basic quantum operation in a classical environment:

python

```
from qiskit import QuantumCircuit, Aer, execute

# Create a quantum circuit with one qubit
qc = QuantumCircuit(1)

# Apply a Hadamard gate to the qubit
qc.h(0)

# Measure the qubit
qc.measure_all()

# Simulate the quantum circuit
simulator = Aer.get_backend('qasm_simulator')
result = execute(qc, simulator).result()

# Display the result
counts = result.get_counts(qc)
print(counts)
```

In this example, the quantum **Hadamard gate** is applied to a qubit, creating a superposition. The result of the simulation would show a 50/50 probability of the qubit being in state 0 or 1.

While this code runs on a classical machine, it mimics the behavior of quantum operations. As quantum hardware improves, low-level quantum programming will likely require more sophisticated tools to directly manipulate quantum bits, similar to how assembly code interacts with classical hardware.

---

4. Hands-On Example: Writing Assembly for a Quantum Simulation on a Classical Machine

Let's create an example where we simulate a **simple quantum circuit** using classical assembly. While we can't run true quantum operations on a classical machine, we can simulate the behavior of qubits and gates in a way that gives us insight into quantum computing.

For simplicity, let's simulate the behavior of a **quantum NOT gate** (equivalent to a classical **bit flip**) using assembly on a classical machine.

4.1 Assembly Code for Simulating a Quantum NOT Gate

```assembly
section .data
    qubit db 0 ; Initialize the qubit state (0)

section .text
    global _start

_start:
    ; Apply a NOT gate (flip the qubit)
    xor byte [qubit], 1    ; Flip the qubit (0 -> 1, 1 -> 0)

    ; Print the result
    mov al, [qubit]        ; Load the qubit state into AL
    add al, '0'            ; Convert 0/1 to '0'/'1'
    mov [output], al       ; Store the result in memory

    ; Exit the program
    mov eax, 1             ; sys_exit
    xor ebx, ebx           ; exit code 0
    int 0x80

section .data
    output db 0            ; Memory location to store result
```

This Assembly code simulates the behavior of a quantum **NOT gate** by flipping the state of a qubit (represented as a single bit in memory). The output will be either 0 or 1, showing how a quantum bit (or qubit) can be manipulated.

Conclusion

As the field of computing continues to evolve, **Assembly language** will continue to play a vital role, especially in **performance-critical** applications, **systems programming**, and **embedded systems**. While high-level languages dominate modern development, **Assembly** remains a powerful tool for developers who need fine-grained control over hardware resources.

This chapter explored the **decline of pure Assembly** in the context of the rise of high-level languages, the impact of **virtualization and containers**, and the exciting future of low-level programming in the realm of **quantum computing**. With the rise of **quantum machines** and **simulators**, the need for low-level control is shifting to an entirely new domain, offering fresh challenges and opportunities for **Assembly programmers**.

Ultimately, while **Assembly** might not be as widespread as it once was, it is far from obsolete. As technologies like **quantum computing** evolve, **Assembly** will continue to play a critical role in understanding and harnessing the true power of modern hardware. The hands-on examples we've covered in this chapter show that low-level programming remains integral to the future of computing, both for classical systems and the emerging world of quantum machines.

CHAPTER 14: REAL-WORLD CASE STUDIES IN LOW-LEVEL PROGRAMMING

Introduction

Low-level programming, particularly through **Assembly language** and **machine code**, has played a pivotal role in shaping the modern computing landscape. While high-level languages have taken center stage in many software development environments due to their ease of use, low-level programming continues to be indispensable in industries where performance, control, and efficiency are paramount. In this chapter, we will explore how low-level programming has transformed several key industries, including **manufacturing, robotics, gaming**, and **healthcare**. We will also look at real-world case studies that highlight how **Assembly** and **machine language** are applied in these sectors, and how their use has evolved over time.

Additionally, we will analyze a **real-world application** of low-level programming in a professional environment to illustrate its practical relevance. From early computing systems to modern-day applications, we will trace the evolution of Assembly language and demonstrate its enduring impact on the world of technology.

1. Low-Level Programming in Industries: Manufacturing, Robotics, Gaming, and Healthcare

1.1 Low-Level Programming in Manufacturing

In **manufacturing**, low-level programming plays a vital role in controlling and automating complex machinery, ensuring that processes run efficiently, safely, and with precision. Manufacturing systems rely heavily on **real-time computing** and **embedded systems**, where low-level code is crucial for handling hardware interactions directly.

In industries like **automated assembly lines** and **CNC (Computer Numerical Control) machines**, **Assembly language** is often used to fine-tune machine operation, allowing engineers to control motion, timing, and precision. These systems often rely on specialized **microcontrollers** or **digital signal processors (DSPs)**, where the low-level control provided by Assembly programming is essential for performance.

CASE STUDY: CNC MACHINES IN MANUFACTURING

CNC machines are used to cut, mill, or shape materials with incredible precision. The controllers that power these machines often run on **embedded systems** that are programmed using low-level languages, including Assembly. For instance, a CNC machine's **stepper motor** control and **toolpath calculations** require direct interaction with hardware components, which is achieved through Assembly programming.

In the early days of CNC machines, engineers would program the control systems using Assembly to handle motor movements and timing. Today, while many CNC systems use higher-level languages, low-level programming remains an essential tool for optimizing machine performance, ensuring **real-time control** and efficient use of resources.

1.2 Low-Level Programming in Robotics

The field of **robotics** relies heavily on low-level programming to achieve precise control over mechanical systems. Robotics combines complex hardware, sensors, and actuators, all of which require real-time interaction with software. Low-level programming in **Assembly** allows robotics engineers to fine-tune the **motion control algorithms, sensor data processing**, and **actuator responses**, ensuring smooth and accurate operation.

Robots in applications such as **industrial automation, surgical assistance**, and **military defense systems** rely on **embedded microcontrollers** programmed in low-level languages to handle critical tasks like **path planning, feedback control**, and **real-time decision-making**.

CASE STUDY: ROBOTIC ARMS IN MANUFACTURING

Robotic arms used in assembly lines, particularly in automotive manufacturing, are an excellent example of low-level programming in robotics. These arms perform tasks like welding, painting, and material handling with high precision. The motion of these robotic arms is controlled by **real-time systems** that rely on low-level programming to execute complex operations with high speed and accuracy.

For example, the **inverse kinematics** required to position the arm's end effector at precise angles involves mathematical calculations and direct control over the motors. Writing this control in high-level languages would introduce unnecessary overhead, so engineers often use Assembly to ensure that each movement is executed as efficiently as possible.

1.3 Low-Level Programming in Gaming

In the world of **gaming**, low-level programming has traditionally been the key to optimizing performance and making the most of hardware capabilities. While modern game engines are largely written in **C++** and higher-level languages, **Assembly** was once at the core of game development, particularly in the days of **8-bit** and **16-bit consoles**.

Even in modern games, low-level programming remains crucial for optimizing performance in areas such as **graphics rendering**, **collision detection**, and **real-time physics simulations**. Game developers use **Assembly language** to write **custom shaders**, **optimized rendering pipelines**, and **hardware-accelerated graphics**, which are essential for achieving high frame rates and visual fidelity.

CASE STUDY: EARLY VIDEO GAME CONSOLES

Early video game consoles, such as the **Atari 2600** and the **Nintendo Entertainment System (NES)**, had very limited processing power and memory. Game developers had to write code in **Assembly language** to maximize the performance of these machines. For example, developers of the NES used **6502 Assembly** to write fast, memory-efficient code that rendered 2D graphics and handled player input in real-time.

The limitations of these consoles meant that developers had to squeeze every bit of performance out of the hardware. Today, while higher-level languages are more common in game development, **Assembly** remains important in **game optimization**, particularly in **graphics programming** and **real-time rendering**.

1.4 Low-Level Programming in Healthcare

In the **healthcare** industry, low-level programming is essential for the development of medical devices, particularly those that require precise control over sensors and actuators. **Embedded systems** in healthcare devices, such as **pacemakers**, **insulin pumps**, and **MRI machines**, rely on low-level programming to interact directly with hardware components and ensure the safety and efficacy of medical procedures.

CASE STUDY: PACEMAKERS AND MEDICAL IMPLANTS

A **pacemaker** is a medical device that regulates a patient's heartbeat by sending electrical impulses to the heart. These devices must operate with high reliability, accuracy, and power efficiency. The **microcontrollers** inside pacemakers are often programmed in **Assembly language** to handle real-time monitoring of the heart's electrical activity, manage communication with external devices, and ensure that the pacemaker responds appropriately to detected anomalies.

Low-level programming ensures that these devices can function in real-time and with extremely low power consumption. Since these devices must operate reliably for long periods without user intervention, optimizing every aspect of their code in **Assembly** is essential for longevity and performance.

2. How Low-Level Programming Transformed These Industries: Real-Life Examples of Assembly and Machine Language Applications

Low-level programming has significantly transformed several industries by enabling systems that operate efficiently and reliably at a very granular level. In manufacturing, robotics, gaming, and healthcare, Assembly and machine code provide the foundation for real-time control, hardware optimization, and high performance.

2.1 Assembly in Manufacturing: Enabling Precision and Efficiency

Manufacturing, particularly in **automated systems** and **robotic control**, has benefited greatly from low-level programming. **Assembly language** allows engineers to write code that interacts directly with hardware components, minimizing the overhead introduced by high-level abstractions. The result is highly optimized systems capable of achieving high precision and efficiency in manufacturing processes.

For instance, in **CNC machining**, Assembly language allows for precise control of motors, sensors, and actuators, ensuring that each cut, weld, or component placement is executed with the utmost accuracy. This level of control cannot be achieved with high-level languages due to the need for low-level hardware manipulation and time-critical execution.

2.2 Robotics and Real-Time Control: Precision in Motion

The field of robotics has also been greatly transformed by low-level programming. Robots, whether they are industrial robots or medical devices like **surgical robots**, require real-time control over their movements, sensors, and interactions with the environment. Low-level programming in **Assembly** ensures that the timing and precision required for these systems are achieved.

For example, in **autonomous robots** used for industrial inspection or delivery, **Assembly language** is used to manage sensor data processing, decision-making algorithms, and actuator control, all in real-time. This enables robots to react quickly to changes in the environment, making them more efficient and effective.

2.3 Gaming: Pushing the Boundaries of Graphics and Performance

Gaming, particularly in the **early days of video game development**, relied heavily on low-level programming to achieve the best possible performance. Early game consoles, which had very limited computing power, required developers to write optimized assembly code to run games efficiently. The **Atari 2600**, for example, had only 128 bytes of RAM, so game developers had to carefully manage memory and optimize every bit of code to ensure smooth gameplay.

While modern gaming has evolved with more powerful hardware and higher-level game engines, **Assembly language** remains essential for **game optimization**. For example, the optimization of **game physics**, **AI routines**, and **rendering pipelines** often requires low-level code to take full advantage of modern **GPUs** (Graphics Processing Units) and **CPUs**.

2.4 Healthcare: Ensuring Reliability and Efficiency

In the **healthcare** industry, low-level programming has transformed the design of **medical devices** that must operate with a high degree of reliability and precision. For devices like **pacemakers,** **defibrillators,** and **insulin pumps,** low-level code is crucial for interacting with hardware components, managing real-time data from sensors, and ensuring the device functions as expected in life-critical situations.

For example, in a **pacemaker,** the assembly code directly interacts with the heart's electrical signals and adjusts the device's behavior accordingly. The need for low-level control is imperative because even a small delay or error in response time can have serious consequences for the patient's health.

3. The Evolution of Assembly: From Early Computing to Modern-Day Applications

Assembly language has come a long way since its inception in the early days of computing. Initially, assembly was the primary means of programming, as high-level languages like **Fortran** and **Lisp** had not yet been developed. Over time, however, higher-level languages gained prominence due to their portability and ease of use. Despite this shift, the need for low-level programming has persisted, and Assembly continues to play an important role in systems where performance, hardware control, and efficiency are paramount.

3.1 The Birth of Assembly Language

The origins of Assembly language can be traced back to the early 1950s, when programmers began using symbolic representations of machine code to make programming easier. Before this, programmers wrote directly in **machine language** (binary code), which was error-prone and difficult to understand. Assembly language allowed programmers to use human-readable mnemonics like MOV, ADD, and JMP to represent machine instructions, simplifying the development process.

3.2 The Rise of High-Level Languages

As computers grew more powerful, the demand for more abstract and user-friendly programming languages led to the development of high-level languages like **Fortran**, **COBOL**, and later **C**. These languages offered greater portability, meaning that programs could be written once and run on different types of machines without modification. With the introduction of these languages, the role of Assembly shifted from being the primary language for programming to a tool used for optimization and system-level programming.

3.3 Modern-Day Assembly Applications

Today, **Assembly** is no longer the primary language for general-purpose software development. However, it remains indispensable in areas like **embedded systems, real-time computing**, and **performance optimization**. **Assembly** continues to evolve alongside modern computing systems, with new optimizations and techniques for interacting with the latest hardware, such as **SIMD (Single Instruction, Multiple Data)** and **GPU programming**.

Modern processors, like those used in **mobile devices, gaming consoles**, and **data centers**, require low-level control and optimization that only Assembly can provide. For example, **SIMD extensions** in **x86** and **ARM** processors allow developers to write **vectorized operations** that process multiple data points simultaneously, improving performance in computationally intensive tasks like image processing, AI, and machine learning.

4. Hands-On Example: Analyzing a Real-World Application of Low-Level Programming in a Professional Environment

To bring everything together, let's analyze a real-world example of **low-level programming** in a professional environment. We'll take the case of **real-time data processing** in **embedded systems**, specifically looking at a system that uses low-level programming to process sensor data in **automated industrial equipment**.

4.1 The System: Real-Time Sensor Data Processing

Imagine a factory floor where **industrial robots** are performing assembly tasks. These robots are equipped with sensors that measure various parameters such as temperature, pressure, and speed. The data collected by these sensors must be processed in **real-time** to ensure that the robot performs its task with precision and accuracy.

The processing system uses an **embedded microcontroller** running low-level code written in **Assembly language** to handle the sensor data. The microcontroller communicates with the sensors via **I2C** or **SPI** protocols, collects data, processes it, and makes real-time adjustments to the robot's movements.

4.2 Assembly Code for Sensor Data Handling

In this case, low-level programming is crucial because the microcontroller must process incoming data from the sensors quickly and efficiently. Here's an example of Assembly code that handles **sensor data acquisition**:

```assembly
assembly

section .data
    sensor_data db 0, 0, 0 ; Buffer to store sensor
data

section .text
    global _start

_start:
    ; Initialize communication with sensor
    ; (Assume that the microcontroller has a
peripheral to handle this)
    call init_sensor

    ; Read sensor data (e.g., from a temperature
sensor)
    call read_sensor_data
    mov al, [sensor_data] ; Load sensor data into
register

    ; Process sensor data (e.g., check if temperature
is within range)
    cmp al, 100             ; Compare the temperature
with threshold value (100)
    jg overheat_detected  ; Jump to overheat handler
if temperature > 100

normal_operation:
    ; Code to handle normal operation
    jmp _start

overheat_detected:
    ; Handle overheating
    ; (e.g., stop the robot, sound alarm, etc.)
    jmp _start
```

4.3 Real-World Benefits of Low-Level Programming

In this real-world scenario, **low-level programming** in Assembly
allows the system to:

- **Minimize latency**: Processing sensor data as quickly as possible to make real-time decisions.
- **Ensure accuracy**: Precise control over sensor interactions ensures that the data is read and processed correctly.
- **Optimize performance**: Assembly allows for tight control over memory usage and processing power, ensuring the system runs efficiently in a constrained environment.

This is just one example of how low-level programming is used in professional environments to optimize performance and ensure reliability. In industries where precision and real-time processing are essential, **Assembly language** continues to be a valuable tool for engineers and developers.

Conclusion

Low-level programming, particularly through **Assembly language** and **machine code**, continues to be a vital part of modern computing. While high-level languages dominate general software development, **Assembly** remains indispensable in industries like **manufacturing, robotics, gaming**, and **healthcare**, where performance, precision, and real-time processing are critical. Through real-world case studies, we've seen how **Assembly** enables fine-grained control over hardware and how it remains essential for optimizing performance in specialized fields.

From its origins as the primary method for programming to its modern-day role in optimizing performance, **Assembly language** has undergone significant evolution. Today, it coexists with high-level languages and remains a powerful tool in the hands of developers and engineers who need to maximize system efficiency. As new technologies like **quantum computing** emerge, **low-level**

programming will continue to play a key role in shaping the future of computing, proving that even in an era of abstraction, there is still a place for **direct hardware control.**

CHAPTER 15: FINAL PROJECT: BUILDING A LOW-LEVEL APPLICATION

Introduction

Building a low-level application from scratch provides an opportunity to apply the knowledge gained throughout this book about **Assembly, machine language**, and **systems programming**. In this chapter, we will walk through the process of developing a **complex low-level application**, covering everything from initial planning to execution. We will also discuss various **optimization techniques** that can improve the performance and memory usage of the application, followed by methods for **testing and debugging** low-level code to ensure it functions as expected.

To bring these concepts to life, we will build and test a **custom low-level application**. The project example will involve developing a simple **hardware controller** or a basic **operating system**. The hands-on approach will help reinforce your understanding of how low-level programming works in real-world environments.

1. Project Overview: A Hands-On Project to Build a Complex Low-Level Application

1.1 Why Build a Low-Level Application?

Building a low-level application serves several purposes:

- **Practical experience**: You will gain direct experience in controlling hardware, managing memory, and interacting with the CPU using Assembly and machine language.
- **Performance optimization**: Low-level programming allows you to optimize for performance, memory usage, and efficiency, which is critical in resource-constrained environments.
- **Understanding hardware interaction**: You'll better understand how software interfaces with the hardware, which is essential for tasks like operating systems, embedded systems, and real-time applications.

Low-level applications require careful management of system resources and direct communication with hardware. Whether you are developing a **hardware controller**, a **real-time system**, or even a **basic operating system**, the principles of Assembly and machine language programming are fundamental to their design and operation.

1.2 Project Objective

In this project, we will build a **custom low-level application** that interfaces with hardware or manages system resources. Our goal is to create something tangible that can interact with the hardware at a low level, providing insight into how low-level programming is used in real-world applications. Depending on your interest, this could be:

- A **simple operating system** that can boot, load programs, and provide basic services (like memory management and input/output).
- A **hardware controller** that interfaces with sensors, motors, or other components, performing specific tasks like reading sensor data or controlling a motor based on inputs.

2. Step-by-Step Guide: From Initial Planning to Execution

2.1 Step 1: Initial Planning

Before jumping into coding, it's essential to **plan** the application thoroughly. Building a low-level application requires careful consideration of the system architecture, resources, and goals. Here's how to approach the planning phase:

- **Define the Scope**: Determine the functionality of the application. Will it be a **barebones operating system** that can manage a few basic tasks? Or will it be a **device driver** or **hardware controller** for managing peripherals like sensors, motors, or displays?
- **Determine the Hardware Requirements**: Identify the hardware on which the application will run. This could be a **microcontroller**, **Raspberry Pi**, or a virtual machine. Understanding the hardware is crucial because low-level programming involves writing code that directly interacts with this hardware.
- **Choose the Language**: While the focus of this chapter is on low-level programming with **Assembly**, consider whether you will need to use other languages (like **C**) for parts of the application. Many low-level applications use **C** for higher-level abstractions, with critical code written in **Assembly** for optimization.
- **System Architecture**: Decide on the architecture of your system. If you are building a simple operating system, you'll need to plan out the memory model, interrupt handling, and hardware initialization. If you're building a hardware controller, you'll need to determine how the controller will interface with sensors and actuators.

2.2 Step 2: Setting Up the Development Environment

Once you've defined the project scope and system architecture, it's time to set up your **development environment**. For low-level applications, this typically involves:

- **Assembler and Compiler**: Choose an assembler (like **NASM** or **GAS**) to write your Assembly code. If you're using C for higher-level logic, set up a C compiler (like **GCC** or **Clang**).
- **Linker and Debugger**: You'll need a linker to combine your object files into an executable and a debugger like **GDB** to help debug your code. If you're working with hardware, you may also need tools like **OpenOCD** or **JTAG** debuggers to interact with microcontrollers or embedded systems.
- **Hardware/Emulator Setup**: If you're targeting real hardware, make sure you have access to the necessary development boards or devices. Alternatively, for testing on a virtual machine, set up an emulator like **QEMU** for a more controlled environment.

2.3 Step 3: Writing the Core Application Code

The core of any low-level application is the **system initialization** and **hardware control**. Let's look at two example projects: a **simple operating system** and a **hardware controller**.

EXAMPLE 1: WRITING A SIMPLE OPERATING SYSTEM

To write a basic operating system, we would start by writing **bootloader code** that loads the OS into memory and prepares the system to execute. Here's a basic breakdown of the steps involved:

1. **Bootloader**: This code is responsible for setting up the system after the computer or embedded device powers up. It

initializes the CPU, loads the kernel into memory, and transfers control to the kernel.

2. **Memory Management**: Write code to manage memory allocation for the OS. This includes setting up a **heap** and a **stack**.

3. **System Calls**: Implement basic system calls for interacting with the hardware, such as reading input from the keyboard, writing to the screen, and managing simple file operations.

4. **Interrupt Handling**: Write code to handle **hardware interrupts** (such as timer interrupts or keyboard input), which allows the OS to respond to hardware events in real-time.

EXAMPLE 2: WRITING A HARDWARE CONTROLLER

To write a hardware controller, you would need to interface with peripherals such as **sensors**, **displays**, or **actuators**. Here are the basic steps:

1. **Initialization**: Write code to initialize the hardware peripherals, including configuring the necessary registers and communication protocols (e.g., **SPI, I2C**, or **UART**).

2. **Sensor Data Handling**: Write routines to read data from sensors (e.g., temperature or pressure sensors) and process that data for use in controlling the hardware.

3. **Control Logic**: Implement logic to make decisions based on sensor input, such as adjusting the speed of a motor or activating a relay.

4. **Communication**: Implement communication protocols (e.g., **UART** for serial communication) to send data between the controller and other devices.

2.4 Step 4: Testing and Debugging

Once you've written the core code, it's time to test and debug your application. Low-level programming often involves dealing with hardware that doesn't behave the same way every time, so debugging is especially important.

- **Testing on Real Hardware**: If you're working with real hardware, make sure to test your application in small steps, verifying that each part of the system (e.g., peripheral initialization, memory management, etc.) works correctly.
- **Unit Testing**: For each piece of functionality, write unit tests that simulate hardware interactions. You can use **QEMU** or other emulators to run your tests in a controlled environment before deploying them to real hardware.
- **Debugging**: Use debugging tools like **GDB** or **JTAG** debuggers to trace through your code, monitor register values, and identify problems like memory corruption or improper register usage.

2.5 Step 5: Optimization

Once your application is working, the next step is optimization. Low-level applications often have to make efficient use of limited resources like **CPU cycles**, **memory**, and **power**.

- **Performance Optimization**: Optimize your Assembly code for performance by using efficient instructions, minimizing branching, and ensuring that registers are used as much as possible to avoid memory access.
- **Memory Optimization**: Minimize memory usage by using efficient data structures, freeing memory when it is no longer needed, and ensuring that memory is allocated and deallocated properly.

- **Power Efficiency**: For embedded applications, power efficiency is critical. Write code that minimizes the power consumption of the system by turning off unused peripherals, using low-power modes, and optimizing the timing of operations.

3. Optimization Techniques: How to Improve Performance and Memory Usage

Optimizing low-level applications is an essential skill for any systems programmer. The most common areas of optimization in low-level programming are **performance** and **memory usage**.

3.1 Performance Optimization

- **Instruction Efficiency**: Assembly allows you to control the exact instructions that the CPU executes. Use the most efficient instructions available for the task at hand. For example, using **MOV** instead of **PUSH/POP** when transferring data between registers can reduce instruction overhead.
- **Loop Unrolling**: If you are performing repetitive operations, consider unrolling loops to reduce the overhead of branching. For example, instead of a loop that runs 10 times, manually write out the 10 iterations to eliminate the need for repeated comparisons.

3.2 Memory Usage Optimization

Memory optimization in low-level applications is especially important in **embedded systems** where resources are limited. Here are some techniques for optimizing memory usage:

- **Memory Pooling**: Instead of allocating and deallocating memory dynamically, use a memory pool to manage memory more efficiently.
- **Stack and Heap Management**: Use the stack for small, short-lived variables and the heap for larger, more complex objects. Ensure that the heap is managed carefully to avoid fragmentation.
- **Data Packing**: Use **bit fields** or **bitwise operations** to pack data into the smallest memory spaces possible, especially when working with flags or status indicators.

---

4. Testing and Debugging: Ensuring Your Low-Level Application Works as Expected

Testing and debugging low-level applications can be challenging due to the direct interaction with hardware and the lack of high-level abstractions. However, effective testing and debugging are crucial to ensure that your application functions as expected.

4.1 Unit Testing

While it's harder to automate testing in low-level programming, you can still write **unit tests** to verify the correctness of individual components. For example, if you're writing code to control a sensor, write tests to check if the sensor is being initialized correctly and whether the data returned is within expected ranges.

4.2 Debugging Techniques

Low-level debugging often requires tools like **GDB, JTAG**, or **hardware simulators**. These tools allow you to inspect the registers, memory, and control flow of your application. Key techniques include:

- **Breakpoints**: Set breakpoints to pause the program at specific locations and inspect the state of the system.
- **Watchpoints**: Set watchpoints to track changes to variables or memory locations in real-time.
- **Step Execution**: Step through your code one instruction at a time to examine how the program is executing and where things may be going wrong.

---

5. Hands-On Example: Build and Test a Custom Low-Level Application

Now, let's build a custom low-level application from scratch. We'll create a **simple hardware controller** for an embedded system, such as a microcontroller, that reads input from a **sensor** and controls an **LED** based on the sensor value.

5.1 The Hardware Setup

Let's assume that we have a simple microcontroller (e.g., **Arduino**, **Raspberry Pi**, or any microcontroller with basic I/O capabilities). The sensor we're using will be a **temperature sensor**, and we will control an LED to indicate whether the temperature is within a safe range.

5.2 Writing the Code

Here's an outline of the assembly code:

1. **Initialize the sensor.**
2. **Read the sensor value** (temperature).
3. **Compare the sensor value** to a threshold.
4. **Control the LED** based on the comparison.

The code will look like this:

```assembly
assembly

; Initialize Sensor and LED
mov r0, #0x00    ; Address of the sensor
mov r1, #0x01    ; Address of the LED

; Read Sensor Value
read_sensor:
    in r2, [r0]  ; Read sensor value into register r2

; Compare Sensor Value
    cmp r2, #30   ; Compare sensor value with
threshold (30 degrees)
    jge above_threshold ; If greater than or equal,
jump to above_threshold

; Below threshold: Turn on LED
below_threshold:
    out r1, #1    ; Turn on LED
    jmp end

; Above threshold: Turn off LED
above_threshold:
    out r1, #0    ; Turn off LED

end:
    ; End of program
```

5.3 Testing the Application

Once the code is written, upload it to the microcontroller and test it with the sensor. You should be able to see the LED turn on when the temperature is below the threshold and turn off when it exceeds the threshold.

Conclusion

In this chapter, we built a **custom low-level application** from scratch, focusing on the process from initial planning to execution. We discussed the importance of **optimization** for both performance and memory usage and explored techniques for **testing and debugging** low-level applications. Through the hands-on example, we demonstrated how to write and test a low-level application that interfaces with hardware, specifically controlling an LED based on sensor input.

Low-level programming may seem daunting at first, but it provides unparalleled control over system resources, making it an invaluable skill in various fields, from embedded systems to operating systems and hardware development. By understanding and applying the techniques covered in this chapter, you are well on your way to mastering low-level programming and creating efficient, powerful applications.

CONCLUSION

Introduction

As we close the final chapter of this journey into low-level programming, it's an excellent time to reflect on the invaluable knowledge you've gained throughout this book. Whether you've come to this field with a background in high-level programming or have started from scratch, low-level programming offers a profound understanding of how computers work at the most fundamental level. From **Assembly language** to **machine code**, **hardware control**, and **performance optimization**, we've explored the intricacies of low-level code that make your software closer to the machine and significantly more efficient.

In this conclusion, we will **reflect on the key takeaways** from the book, providing a summary of the concepts covered, reinforcing the importance of low-level programming, and offering practical guidance for your next steps in the world of Assembly and machine language. We'll discuss the **next steps** in your learning journey, encourage further experimentation with low-level code, and suggest resources to deepen your knowledge and continue growing in the field. Low-level programming is a vast and ever-evolving domain, and by taking the next steps, you can stay ahead of the curve and continue to develop your skills.

1. Reflecting on What You've Learned: Summarizing the Key Takeaways

Throughout this book, we've explored a broad range of topics that lay the foundation for understanding and mastering **low-level programming**. Here's a recap of the core areas you've learned:

1.1 Introduction to Low-Level Programming

In the early chapters, we explored **low-level programming fundamentals,** starting with an introduction to **Assembly language** and how it connects to **machine code.** You learned how computers interpret and execute instructions, with a detailed focus on how **Assembly language** operates at the level of the CPU and memory. The concepts of **binary, hexadecimal, instruction sets,** and **CPU registers** were introduced, providing you with the necessary foundation to dive deeper into Assembly.

1.2 Low-Level Security and Exploits

You also learned how low-level programming is closely tied to **security vulnerabilities**. Concepts like **buffer overflows, stack smashing**, and **return-oriented programming (ROP)** were discussed in detail, helping you understand how malicious actors exploit low-level vulnerabilities in software. Importantly, we also covered **defensive programming** techniques, showing you how to write **secure Assembly code** to prevent these exploits and build safe, reliable software.

1.3 Optimizing Low-Level Code

The book also covered performance optimization techniques—one of the key advantages of low-level programming. From **memory**

management to **instruction-level optimizations,** you learned how to make software more efficient by minimizing resource usage and maximizing speed. Concepts like **loop unrolling, register usage,** and **cache optimization** were explored in detail to help you get the best performance from your hardware. In addition, you learned how to use tools like **profiling, benchmarking,** and **debugging** to identify performance bottlenecks and resolve issues in your low-level code.

1.4 Practical Examples and Hands-On Projects

Throughout the book, we introduced **hands-on projects** that demonstrated the practical applications of low-level programming. From creating **simple operating systems** to developing **hardware controllers,** you applied your knowledge of **Assembly** to real-world scenarios. These projects provided a great way to practice coding in low-level environments and get an understanding of how Assembly can be used for controlling hardware, managing system resources, and optimizing code.

1.5 Interfacing with High-Level Languages

One of the most powerful aspects of low-level programming is its ability to interface with higher-level languages. You learned how to combine **C/C++** with **Assembly** using **inline assembly** and **linking assembly with C code,** enabling you to write hybrid programs that leverage the strengths of both worlds. This skill is invaluable in areas like performance optimization, embedded systems, and systems programming, where direct hardware control is necessary but high-level features are still desired.

1.6 The Future of Low-Level Programming

Finally, we explored the future of low-level programming. You learned how **virtualization** and **containers** are changing the way low-level code interacts with hardware. We also touched on emerging fields like **quantum computing**, where low-level programming is still essential for controlling and simulating quantum systems. Understanding these evolving trends ensures that you're prepared for the next wave of technological advancements and gives you a glimpse into how low-level programming will continue to evolve.

2. Next Steps: Encouraging Readers to Continue Experimenting with Low-Level Code

While this book has provided you with a solid foundation in low-level programming, the journey doesn't end here. In fact, this is just the beginning of your exploration into the world of **Assembly** and **machine language**. As with any complex skill, the key to mastery is practice and experimentation. Here's how you can continue your learning journey:

2.1 Experiment with Real-World Projects

One of the most effective ways to deepen your understanding of low-level programming is to work on real-world projects. By writing more complex programs, you can solidify the concepts you've learned and expand your skillset. Some ideas for real-world projects include:

- **Developing a simple operating system**: Start by writing a **bootloader** and a basic **kernel** that can handle memory management and I/O operations. This project will give you hands-on experience in how an OS interacts with hardware.
- **Building an embedded system**: Work with microcontrollers (like **Arduino** or **Raspberry Pi**) and write low-level code to interface with sensors, actuators, and other hardware. You could build a small hardware controller or a simple **IoT device**.
- **Optimizing an existing application**: Take an existing C or C++ program and optimize the performance by writing performance-critical sections in **Assembly**. Focus on improving memory usage, speed, and responsiveness.

2.2 Use Online Platforms for Hands-On Practice

Several online platforms provide environments where you can practice low-level programming and improve your skills:

- **Online Assemblers and Emulators**: Websites like **onlinegdb**, **JDoodle**, or **replit** allow you to experiment with Assembly and simulate real hardware behavior. These platforms are great for testing small snippets of Assembly code without needing physical hardware.
- **Challenge Platforms**: Participate in coding challenges and competitions on platforms like **LeetCode**, **HackerRank**, or **Codeforces**, where low-level optimizations are often necessary for solving complex problems.

2.3 Explore Advanced Topics in Low-Level Programming

As you become more comfortable with the basics, you can begin exploring more advanced topics in low-level programming, such as:

- **Advanced system-level programming**: Learn more about **kernel development, device drivers**, and **inter-process communication**. These topics require a deeper understanding of how operating systems manage resources and interact with hardware.
- **Real-time and embedded systems programming**: Explore how real-time systems work and how to write code for **embedded systems** with strict timing and performance requirements.
- **Optimization for modern architectures**: Dive into **SIMD programming, GPU programming**, and **multithreading**, which are essential for writing high-performance applications that make the most of modern hardware.

2.4 Join Low-Level Programming Communities

Being part of a community can provide invaluable support as you continue learning. Joining forums, contributing to open-source projects, and attending meetups can expose you to a wide range of ideas and practices. Some active communities include:

- **Stack Overflow**: Participate in discussions about low-level programming and ask questions when you encounter challenges.
- **GitHub**: Contribute to open-source projects that involve low-level code or start your own projects. Engaging in collaborative projects will accelerate your learning and expose you to more experienced programmers.
- **Reddit**: Subreddits like r/embedded, r/assembly, and r/sysadmin are great places to find resources, tutorials, and discussions about low-level programming.

3. Building on Your Knowledge: Resources for Further Learning and Community Involvement

Now that you've gained a solid foundation in low-level programming, there are numerous resources to help you continue building on this knowledge and stay current in the field.

3.1 Books and Courses for Further Learning

Books and online courses can offer in-depth knowledge on specific aspects of low-level programming. Some recommended resources include:

- **Books:**
    - *"Programming from the Ground Up"* by Jonathan Bartlett: A comprehensive guide to Assembly programming and systems-level development.
    - *"The Art of Assembly Language"* by Randall Hyde: An in-depth exploration of Assembly language with a focus on the x86 architecture.
    - *"Modern Operating Systems"* by Andrew Tanenbaum: Learn about the internal workings of operating systems and how low-level programming fits into system design.
- **Online Courses:**
    - **Coursera**: Offers courses in low-level programming, operating systems, and embedded systems programming from universities like **Stanford** and **Princeton**.
    - **Udemy**: Provides affordable courses on Assembly language, embedded systems, and system-level programming.

- o **edX**: Take free courses from **MIT** and **Harvard** on operating systems, security, and low-level programming.

3.2 Specialized Forums and Websites

To continue your learning and stay updated on industry trends, check out these specialized forums and websites:

- **Stack Overflow**: A go-to forum for troubleshooting low-level programming issues and engaging with other developers.
- **GitHub**: Explore open-source low-level projects to see how others write Assembly code and contribute to those projects.
- **Reddit**: Subreddits like r/embedded, r/assembly, r/compsci, and r/linux are excellent for learning and discussing low-level programming topics.

3.3 Conferences and Meetups

Attending conferences and meetups can help you stay at the forefront of low-level programming. Here are some notable events to consider:

- **DEF CON**: A massive cybersecurity and hacking conference, where you can learn about **exploit development, reverse engineering,** and other low-level topics.
- **Embedded Systems Conference (ESC)**: Focuses on embedded system development, with topics on **microcontrollers, real-time systems,** and low-level programming.
- **The Assembly Language Programming Meetup**: An informal meetup for programmers interested in learning more about Assembly and low-level system programming.

Conclusion: Keep Pushing the Boundaries of Low-Level Programming

This book has taken you through the essentials of low-level programming and its role in modern computing. You've learned the intricacies of **Assembly language**, **machine code**, and **systems programming**, along with the skills to build, optimize, and test real-world low-level applications. Whether you are developing **embedded systems**, working on **operating systems**, or simply interested in improving your performance-critical applications, you now possess the knowledge and skills to move forward confidently.

However, the world of **low-level programming** is vast and constantly evolving. Technologies such as **quantum computing**, **AI hardware accelerators**, and **real-time systems** continue to push the boundaries of what low-level code can do. So, your journey doesn't end here. It's time to continue experimenting, building, and engaging with the community to continue expanding your knowledge.

Low-level programming may be more challenging than high-level coding, but it provides a level of **control**, **efficiency**, and **performance** that you can't achieve with any other approach. The skills you've acquired here will serve you well as you embark on new projects, tackle more advanced topics, and contribute to cutting-edge technologies.

So, keep coding, keep experimenting, and never stop learning. The world of low-level programming is waiting for you to shape it.

www.ingramcontent.com/pod-product-compliance
Lightning Source LLC
LaVergne TN
LVHW022345060326
832902LV00022B/4247